CHINA MY LOVE

The Story of Florence Logan

as told to

Patricia Burke Young

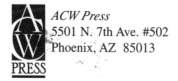
ACW Press
5501 N. 7th Ave. #502
Phoenix, AZ 85013

Publisher's Cataloging-in-Publication
(Provided by Quality Books, Inc.)

Logan, Florence Leila, 1897-1997
    China my love : the story of Florence Logan / as told
to Patricia Burke Young — 1st ed.
    p. cm.
    ISBN 1-892525-08-9

    1. Logan, Florence Leila, 1897-1997 2. Presbyterian
Church in the U.S.A.--Missions--China--Biography
3. Women missionaries--China--Biography.
4. Missionaries--China--Biography. 5. Women
missionaries--United States--Biography. 6. Missionaries
United States--Biography   I. Young, Patricia Burke
II. Title

BV3427.L64A3 1999   266/.5151/092
  [B]   QBI98-990018

Printed in the United States of America

To obtain more copies please contact:
Patricia Burke Young
15 Country Road 3777
Farmington, NM 87401
See the order form in the back of this book.

Dedicated to Lorna Logan,
without whose help this book
would not have been possible

Acknowledgments

I wish to express appreciation to my husband, Willis Young, for all his help, apt suggestions and encouragement; to my son, John Burke, who drove me many times to San Francisco to see Florence Logan; and to Dwight and Agnes Mason Jr., who believed in the book and helped make it possible.

About the Author

Patricia Burke Young, M.A., retired teacher and pastor's wife, is also co-author of "Adventures From God's Word" and recently wrote "The Big Missionary." She is a newspaper columnist, and founder of the "Southwest Christian Writers Association." She lives in Farmington, New Mexico with her husband, Dr. Willis Young, a retired Army Chaplain.

Contents

Part 3

1949-1951: Florence Logan's two-and-a-half year internment in a Communist compound under a completely Marxist regime.

Author's Notes

"We have a letter from Florence," my mother exclaimed. That was the first time I became aware of this remarkable woman called Florence Logan. My eight brothers and sisters, my grandma, and I would listen in fascination as my mother read the latest episode from her cousin who was a missionary to China.

Even as a child I realized that this woman—the only missionary to twenty million Chinese living in the country area surrounding Paotingfu, China—was no ordinary person. That part of China never knew peace during her tumultuous stay, and the war hazards, floods, and famines would have daunted anyone less courageous. But Florence, along with the bands of young people she trained, swept through the countryside, relentlessly attacking idol worship and ignorance, while also teaching the Chinese to worship the true God.

Florence Logan, born January 7, 1897, in Rhodes, Iowa, grew up in Seattle, Washington, where she received her B.A. in journalism from the University of Washington. She served as the first woman editor of the *University of Washington Daily*. After college, counseled by Dr. Mark Matthews, she took postgraduate study in Bible at Moody Institute of Chicago and Biblical Seminary in New York to prepare for foreign mission work.

When Florence went to China at the age of 24, under the Presbyterian Board of Foreign Missions, her headquarters were in the city of Paotingfu. However, she spent her time in small villages where she lived with the country people, wore their clothes, and took part in their lives. During this time, Florence started Bible schools, built churches, provided work for young Chinese, and fed the hungry—a momentous task, even with help.

Her life spanned three eras: 1) The oppressive years under the Chinese Republic and Chiang Kai-shek, during the time of dangerous Chinese warlords and the Japanese taking of Manchuria; 2) years of Japanese aggression and occupation, collapse of the Republic, and Communist uprisings; also of floods, fighting, and famine; and 3) two-and-a-half years that Florence spent in a repressive Communist compound under a completely Marxist regime.

When Japan invaded China, Florence returned to the United States on the exchange slip Gripsholm. She returned to China after two years, however, itinerating in the country and training young people to carry on her work.

Finally, when the Communists took over China, Florence—after 30 years of ministry in China—returned home, only to go back and serve as a missionary in Taiwan for the next 10 years. When she left China, one of the last missionaries to go, she left a legacy that would carry on in the face of opposition just as she herself had—a legacy of young people who would become a strong part of the Chinese church: persecuted, tough, suffering, invincible. Later in Taiwan, Florence and a coworker established the Hsin Chu Bible School and College, which still trains lay people for Christian service. Many of the school's graduates have gone on to become pastors.

After 40 years of missionary service, Florence retired at the age of 65, making her home with her beloved sister Lorna at "The Sequoias" in San Francisco. From there, she continued to write, speak around the country, and teach Bible classes. On March 2, 1997, at the age of 100, she went home to be with the Lord.

I believe Florence's superb descriptions of China, gleaned from her knowledge of China's history—going back to what may be early Christianity under emperors who made sacrifices for the sins of the people— will fascinate the reader. The deep truths she shared from the Bible, as well as her own committed life, speak for themselves. And always, in every situation, Florence gave the glory to God.

P.B.Y.

PART 1

1926-1931:

The years spent under the Chinese
Republic and Chiang Kai-shek; a time of oppression
by Chinese warlords, and of the Japanese
taking of Manchuria.

Florence Logan

CHAPTER 1

IT MUST BE A MISTAKE

"You ought to go to China as a missionary."

I stared at my pastor, Dr. Mark Matthews. "Me, a missionary?" I was shocked at his suggestion. A university graduate, go as a plain missionary? I always believed missionaries to be poorly educated and ineffective, except for doctors and nurses. It was a poor use of good material, I felt, to be singled out for mission work. But although at the time I thought I would be doing something magnificent for the Lord to even consider being a missionary, I was to find out that God was doing something magnificent in giving me the privilege of going.

Later, as I looked back to the events that led up to Dr. Matthew's statement, I wondered, where had the years gone? And why, in my teens, had I acted so contrary? I winced at the memory. I had been impossible, insisting on my "right" to stay home from family excursions so I could enjoy more worldly activities.

Despite my obnoxious attitude, Father had paid my board so I could live near the university I attended. I knew the $40 a month must have been a financial drain.

But then, strangely, the dances and card parties I attended began to lose their allurement; they no longer satisfied. After a time of soul searching, I decided to let God make my plans, instead of doing it myself, and began to look for my social life in the church.

Soon I found it in a Bible class which met Monday nights, attended by about 100 young women. Since World War I had catapulted many of the eligible young men into uniform, most women found themselves dateless.

Meanwhile, as a journalism student at the University of Washington, I became editor of the campus *Daily*, then advanced to the position of reporter for the *Seattle Post Intelligencer*. Upon graduation, I went on staff full time. But God had not forgotten my promise to let Him make my plans, and soon I found newspaper work did not satisfy, either. Then, providentially, the *Intelligencer* had to retrench and, as the saying goes, "The last hired, the first fired," and I lost my job.

This did not disturb me too greatly, because my friends in the Bible class subtly suggested God might be freeing me to attend Bible school in preparation for Christian work. I left Washington to study for a year at Biola Bible College in Los Angeles, then moved to Chicago and studied for a year at Moody Bible Institute.

During these years my thoughts had already begun to focus on China and I joined the China prayer group in each place, never dreaming I would someday go to that country. My practical assignments at Moody in personal work and street evangelism were to become especially helpful for later country work in China.

However, at this time, I hazily surmised God might be preparing me for some type of Christian journalism. But no, the bombshell struck instead on that day when Dr. Matthews called me to his office to confront me with the words: "You ought to go to China as a missionary."

To my surprise, when I applied to the Presbyterian Mission Board, the North China Mission had already requested of them a woman missionary to work in the Paotingfu area of China, and that became my appointment.

But now, as I stared at the huge gray boat gliding into Victoria Harbor—like an enemy, come to wrench me away from all I held dear—I asked myself, What am I doing here? What had I been thinking of to promise I would go?

With the ship bearing down upon me, there I stood, packed and ready to leave home, church, family, friends. Shortly after, the colored paper streamers broke and the boat moved from the dock and out into the bay, carrying me away from all I loved. The enormity of the step overwhelmed me. I felt lost at such dreadful breaking of ties.

But at that moment, in the providence of God, I received my first experience as a missionary of God's loving care and provision—one that would stay with me through times of war, flood, famine, danger, even house arrest under the Japanese. That day, in a singular way, the God who would never once leave nor forsake me, sent His loving reassurance down to me as I stood shivering on the boat deck. He reminded me that this step I took did not originate from my own self at all, but He Himself was the one sending me and I would be perfectly safe.

As God wrapped the comfort and peace of His love around my heart, the ache and fear left. I knew with certainty I would never be homesick again. And I never was.

CHAPTER 2

CHINA AT LAST!

That must be it! Straining my eyes, I barely made out a thin line on the horizon. Our ship, the Empress of Asia, had just left the clear water of the China Sea for the Yellow Sea, named and colored from the silt washed down by the mighty Yangtze River. I sighed as I thought of the 18 days of calm and storm just experienced on the rolling Pacific. At times I had felt so seasick I thought I would die, but then I feared I wouldn't.

Now, with China actually in sight, it seemed our boat had slowed to a crawl. Even after reaching the channel of the broad Whangpu River, we took an exasperating two hours, escorted by tenders, to reach the Shanghai Bund.

Words can't describe the excitement I felt when I saw the smiling group from the mission headquarters in Shanghai waiting on shore to welcome the new missionaries. With dozens of jabbering, gesticulating coolies trying to grab our suitcases, debarking could have tried our patience, but staff members from the Interdenominational Mission Home helped get our hand luggage through customs. Then we drove straight to the home in a Ford, no less.

The mission home would remain my quarters until arrangements could be made for me to attend language school in Peking. I found it to be a welcome haven, providing a wealth of information about the city and travel in China, as well as helping with all sorts of problems which, indeed, I would experience.

As I viewed Shanghai for the first time in awe, the splendid factories and brick buildings astounded me. I did not expect this impressive, modern city. But Shanghai also had its frightening side. When I found myself thrown into the midst of masses of people with strange faces, wearing odd clothes and jabbering in a strange language, I thought, What a lot of foreigners. Then I realized, They are not foreign; I am.

Little did I dream the Lord would take away that "foreignness" and make me one with them, brothers and sisters in His family, so that for the rest of my life I would feel more at home with the Chinese than with Americans. To my surprised delight, God would ease me through "culture shock," enable me to enjoy simple country food, and even give me some fluency in the language. Best of all, I would gain a love and admiration for the Chinese themselves—no longer to be "they," but "we." But that would only come later with time and, for the present, the newness of my surroundings nearly overwhelmed me.

While in Shanghai we had to get our baggage through customs, clear our accounts with the mission treasurer, and, of course, get supplied with Chinese money. This came in rolls of large silver dollars and a bag of small copper coins, worth about one silver dollar to 160 coins. Later we would need to find an experienced missionary to escort us to Peking for language study. Because we would transfer from a coastal steamer to the railroad, a knowledge of Chinese was essential.

For now, however, my new friends showed me to my third floor room at the mission, which could only be reached by winding and devious ways. Three other women shared my quarters, including Dr. Susan Waddell, with whom I had been commissioned in New York by the Board of Foreign Missions. Both of us had crossed the Pacific together and were now bound for language school in Peking. I was delighted to have her company.

That afternoon I experienced my first "tiffin," the convivial Chinese custom of serving refreshments in the middle of the day, consisting of anything, hot or cold. After tiffin, my roommates entered and ordered me to bed.

"It is the way of the Orient," they explained, "to take a siesta in the middle of the day, then make use of the cool of the morning and evening."

Unused to the climate, I gladly obliged, only to be roused by strange, doleful music floating up from the street.

"Come quick!" my friends summoned. "It's a Chinese funeral."

Never could I have imagined anything so unusual as this pagan ritual. Heading the procession marched several bands playing both Chinese and Western instruments. Then came the mourners on foot, wearing rough white garments and headbands. Following these I saw fancy pagoda-like chairs carried on poles. One held a large photograph of the deceased; others held paper images of his concubines meant to be burned at the grave. (I later learned, to my relief, that such treatment did not apply to the concubines themselves, as I had heard. Indeed, I found some were treated well, as in the case of a wealthy man in Peking who, after his conversion to Christianity, separated from his beautiful concubine and sent her to our Bible school in Paotingfu for training.)

Next in the procession, mendicant Buddhist priests paraded in gorgeous red and black robes. Here and there in the parade I spied a roasted pig, but I couldn't tell whether it might be real or just varnished paper-maché. Along with the priests, 30 men carried poles with 10-foot streamers on which large characters extolled the virtues of the deceased. Other streamers bore huge objects which looked to me like brilliantly colored lamp shades decorated with gay fringes.

Finally, the huge coffin itself arrived in an elaborate catafalque, borne on the shoulders of a score of men and followed by countless one-horse cabs filled with female mourners, also in white.

How different this appeared from a Christian funeral I attended years later in Shuntefu, when Richard Jenness, a missionary colleague beloved to the Chinese, died. Chinese mourners were also present then, but wore only white arm bands. Colorful paper flower wreaths and banners in the procession proclaimed the high esteem held for the pastor and teacher. Joyful hymns of resurrection rang out all the way to his grave.

At the church service, rather than wailing, Mrs. Jenness confidently told the assembled crowd: "I know where he has gone. The Lord has called him to himself. 'Except a corn of wheat fall into the earth and die, it abideth alone: but if it die, it bringeth forth much fruit'" (John 12:24).

But that day in Shanghai, witnessing my first Chinese funeral, I could not see into the future; I could only perceive the hopelessness and lostness of the mourners. And as I watched, I wondered, Will these people learn the truth, that God alone gives hope, even in death? Within myself, I renewed my commitment to do everything I could to bring the people of my new, strange country the only living hope, the Lord Jesus Christ.

CHAPTER 3

PERILS OF "RICK RIDING" AND THE CHOLERA BELT

Where on earth were we going? Susan Waddell and I stared at the unfamiliar scene in alarm as our rickshaw threaded ever deeper into the Shanghai traffic. An older missionary had kindly offered to take us shopping and, at first, with our guide in plain view, we found the trip enjoyable. But now she had disappeared into the traffic. Finally, just as we lost all hope, we found ourselves deposited in the right place. What a relief!

But that was not the end of it. At our destination new trials awaited us.

"A dime will suffice," the missionary had informed us earlier, but the rickshaw man made such a fuss we had to give him two. I soon realized that in Shanghai rickshaw drivers always yelled for more money if they spotted a stranger. Also, the more they received the louder they shouted, even though they had already been paid the usual rate. (When I attended the language school in Peking, I found the politeness of the rickshaw men in that city a refreshing change.)

What a strange place, I thought. Unlike Americans, the Chinese sounded so noisy, shouting back and forth about the simplest routine, such as making change. Also, the rickshaw men uttered funny sounds, calling to each other with grunts and groans. Even the shopkeepers sang in a weird fashion.

In one Shanghai shop, Dr. Waddell and I asked for silk, and to our surprise the bright young clerk escorted us down a side street into a silk store. Then, ceremoniously seating us, he asked what kind we wanted. I thought he received a commission for bringing us in, but he sang out, "Two stores, same master." Though he wanted to serve us Chinese tea, we declined, and were cordially bowed out.

"Why not have an ice cream soda?" Susan suggested. On the way to the chocolate shop we couldn't help but notice many long-fingernailed gentlemen and also quite a few women who minced along on miniature bound feet. (Later, when I ministered in the country villages, my girls' evangelistic band and I would teach a song to these victims of the Chinese custom of foot binding, extolling the joys of "natural" feet.)

We drank our soda, but it didn't taste at all American as I had hoped.

Back in the States, the Board had thoughtfully provided each outgoing missionary a list of items we should take. Some were everyday supplies we could easily pick up at a corner grocery, but which would not be available in China. Others were items experienced missionaries felt would safeguard the health of Westerners adjusting to a new climate and lifestyle.

I lacked three items on my list I had not found at home, so I looked for them on our trip that day to Shanghai. I quickly found the first two: a pith hat and a mosquito net, but the third, a cholera belt, was not to be located. "It must not be important," I told Susan, and let it go.

How wrong I was! On my second summer in China, I traveled by train to Chikungshan in Central China to spend my vacation with friends who lived in a dormitory in a Scandinavian mission girls' school. On the train the heat became oppressive and I lay uncovered on my upper bunk where a refreshing little breeze blew. This turned out to be a mistake! Even before leaving the train I became sick and in great pain. Friends had me carried by chair up the mountain to the mission school (this being the usual method even for well people). At the school, a North China Mission colleague, a nurse, cared for me until I recovered.

Later that summer the school had a sale of knitted and embroidered goods made in mission industrial schools. I purchased a sweater and then noticed a small item I didn't recognize—a white wool knitted circlet. Suddenly it dawned on me: it must be a cholera belt! I quickly acquired one and wore it during the hot weather through all my years in China. Never did I experience a return of that painful affliction.

The mosquito net—hung over the bed with the aid of bamboo poles at the corners—proved necessary during the mosquito season. Only occasionally one got inside and squashed on the net, leaving a red blotch. The pith hats eventually went out of use, but along with many Chinese, I learned to automatically raise a black umbrella when I stepped outdoors in summer heat.

But mosquito nets continued to be useful equipment, and that night, after a final bout in Shanghai with a vociferating rickshaw man over the fare, I fell exhausted into my net-equipped bed for a good night's sleep.

CHAPTER 4

ADVENTURES EN ROUTE TO PEKING

Dr. Waddell swept into my room, anxiety written on her usually pleasant face.

"Our plans have changed," she announced breathlessly. "We can't take the train to Peking for language school after all. Heavy rains washed out much of the railway between Shanghai and Peking. Now we have to take the steamer to Chinwangtao and go the rest of the way from there to Peking by rail."

My heart sank as I remembered my last queasy voyage, and I didn't look forward to traveling by boat to Peking. How often I would hear such words while I lived in China: "The road just flooded." "The bridge washed out." "Flood has made the rails impassable." But I knew I had to begin language school as soon as possible, so I began to prepare for the trip.

We finally managed to secure passage on the Kaiping, one of the best steamers going north, and an old China hand helped us transfer our luggage. To my pleasant surprise, three of my Asia acquaintances went along, including a missionary journalist, Dr. Reed, and, of course, Susan Waddell.

After reaching Chinwangtao about 7:30 p.m., we found no train sleepers to be available, so we sent our trunks to the depot, keeping our hand luggage, and spent the night on the boat.

"Florence, how could you manage to sleep through that awful racket?" Susan asked me the next morning. "Didn't you even realize our steamer loaded coal all night?"

I laughingly decided sleeping must be my one accomplishment in the Orient. This pleased the older missionaries, who strongly advised each new worker on the field to be lazy the first year if possible.

As we traveled to the train station, a youngster, wearing, it seemed, nothing in particular, attached himself to our cavalcade, running alongside, making a soft, musical birdlike song. Obviously he was begging, and I would like to have known what the words meant. At the station, a bevy of other beggars greeted us, a sure sign, Dr. Reed said, that we were in the Orient. I later learned the hard way that to give anything to beggars on the street was an invitation to being mobbed and led to real danger.

At the ticket office, food vendors suddenly sprouted from everywhere, peddling apples, grapes, pears, cakes of limitless variety, and cigarettes. Little tin stoves displayed bowls of hot food resembling noodles or strips of fish.

On the train, we found that crowded conditions made the air foul with smoke and odors. Fortunately, by paying the difference, we were allowed to move into first class.

All the way to Peking, our train sped through fields with grazing flocks of sheep, but we also passed countless walled-in courtyards and flat-roofed one-story buildings. To my surprise, I saw only a single two-wheeled ox-drawn cart. Everything else depended on man power: a pole and two baskets. No tool seemed to exist more pretentious than a stick.

I commented on the huge fields of kaoliang, an important crop which grew on canes 10 to 12 feet high, the bushy brown heads containing edible grain. Dr. Reed told us the canes could also be used for fuel, for thatching roofs, and even for making baskets.

At Tientsin, Dr. Wu, an important official in charge of plague prevention work in Manchuria, climbed aboard. He had been sent to help dedicate the Union Medical College and Hospital of the Rockefeller Foundation of Peking, and would meet the Rockefeller party when it arrived. To our pleasure, Dr. Wu presented each lady in our party with a bouquet of red and purple asters with white lilies. The fragrance of the flowers seemed to me a good omen for our stay in Peking.

Of course we were served tiffin on the train. By now, more aware of Oriental custom, Susan and I thought it safest to drink only bottled liquid so I had lemonade.

"It tastes like citrate of magnesia," I confided to Susan. But because I liked that, it didn't matter.

In Peking, after we procured our baggage, and a host of people from the missionary compound met us, we were escorted through the U.S. Legation quarter. Since walls completely encircle Peking, the South City, and the old city, we went through the Water Gate. It had been cut through after the Boxer Rebellion at the demand of the legation people, and still stood on the spot where the soldiers broke through for their relief.

Imposing gray stone buildings, fine paved streets, and bright lights surrounded us in the legation quarter. We travelers were thrilled to see Old Glory flying, while khaki-clad boys guarded the American legation gate.

The main business street to the compound, however, though smooth and wide, was unpaved. The electric lights shone dimly, while oil lamps eerily illuminated the street vendors in front of the open stores.

My first view of the Presbyterian Mission Compound brought tears to my eyes. Observing everything in amazement, I felt I had stepped from China back into the States. In the moonlight, the beautiful trees, shrubs, and green grass looked inviting.

Six of us sat down to dinner in the doctors' home, including Miss Tabor, a lovely girl who had come for evangelistic work and with whom I would live that year. Dinner included soup, chops, potatoes, beets, greens, and tomato salad, along with ice cream and cookies for dessert.

After dinner, my new friends took me to a large, cheery room in a gray stone two story house, where I would live during my year of language school. To my delight, the room had large windows facing east, a bright green rug, and comfortable white furnishings.

I could hardly wait to unpack when my trunks arrived. It seemed wonderful to have things in order once more. Where did that come from? I thought, as I pulled out a lovely blue and white quilt. Then I knew its source—that mother of mine!

After the long voyage on the Asia, my clothes were hopelessly wrinkled so following dinner that evening, I asked how to get them pressed. A Chinese "Boy" as he was called, though he had been with the doctors 18 years, insisted he would be pleased to press them.

"You came a long way to help my people," he told me. "All I can do is iron your clothes."

I thanked him, thinking, He has the best face. How wonderfully, I thought, the Lord had taken care of every step all the way. Not a mishap or unpleasantness. It didn't seem like "missionarying" to me to enjoy such comfort, and I felt privileged to be here for His service. Later, when I found myself with my girls' evangelistic band, sometimes staying in as many as six different villages during nine weeks' time, I would look back with nostalgia to my year at the compound.

The compound was neatly divided into three parts, separated by the narrowest of streets. In the first part stood the church, girls' school, and hospital. Unlike our churches, men sat on one side and women on the other. Men outnumbered women two to one. How different from home, I thought wryly.

Suddenly I noticed about 100 small boys, seated together, and all looking alike in gray cotton uniforms.

"These children come from the 'Christian Rug Factory'," one of the physicians, Dr. Leonard, explained. I listened as their voices rang out "Praise God from whom all blessings flow" from the Doxology. Somewhere I had heard the Chinese could not sing, but their voices sounded good to me.

Next to the gate opening into the compound stood the mysterious gatekeeper's room. I learned that even though he stayed there all night, he was allowed to go home twice a day for meals. Inside the gate stood the proverbial blank wall I would see so often in China, protecting the interior from prying eyes.

In Peking, the chief mode of transportation, apart from rickshaws, were the "Peking Carts." To my discomfort, the one I obtained consisted only of two large wooden wheels and a flat bottom with no springs. Writing to my sister Lorna, I told her, "As I sat on the bottom on a cushion during my first ride, I enjoyed a sensation like going over the rocky road to Dublin."

At intervals along Peking's streets stood wells, where carriers filled wooden tubs and carted them by wheelbarrow.

"Since everyone pays so much a day for water," I added in my letter, "we should not blame the Chinese for not using more. Also, every so often I see two men with wooden pails of water, dipping from them to sprinkle the street. Just as our rickshaw boy approached one he gave a warning call and we barely escaped a shower."

Continuing to see everywhere the blank walls, except for the shops, I became wildly curious to know what lurked inside. I was to find out, sooner than I thought, on a memorable trip to Peking's famous Temple of Heaven.

But of all the sightseeing that day, the best part was arriving home, when we simply stepped out of our rickshaw and ambled into the house, sending the money out with the boy. I recalled how in Shanghai whenever we paid the rickshaw man, he started to fuss. Here, the fixed rate for different distances and time made travel simple and pleasant.

CHAPTER 5

THE ROCKEFELLER CELEBRATION

I woke up excited one morning, remembering that it was the dedication day of the Rockefeller Union Medical College and Hospital. It was a red-letter day, a medical conference, and it seemed everybody I met turned out to be a doctor. One could get the impression M.D.s were as thick as fleas in China, but most had arrived for the grand doings.

One special visitor at the compound, Dr. Mackey of Paotingfu, turned out to be whom I would probably live with the next year after finishing language school. Short and plump, with dark hair, blue eyes, and glasses, she roomed across the hall from me. With three other doctors eating at our table, the rest of us who had no medical degree felt most unimportant.

Meals were meaningful events here. At breakfast someone read a page from the "Daily Light" devotional booklet, then after prayer, the Boy ceremoniously began to bring the food. Sometimes, along with other dishes, we got corn bread, but made with millet instead of corn. Little did I know then that one day, preaching among the villages of Paotingfu, millet would be my only staple, or that from our mission compound in Paotingfu, we would feed simple millet porridge to thousands of starving persons during one of China's worst area famines.

When we reached the celebration at the hospital grounds, Chinese police handed each of us a red card, with a corresponding tag for our rickshaw boy. Thus we could be matched again later.

The vastness and beauty of the place amazed me. Most of the creamy brick buildings soared three stories high, with roofs of colorful Chinese green tile. Beneath each roof ran a brilliantly colored band of Chinese decoration a foot wide, while a similar band encircled the second story, thus delightfully combining Western and Oriental.

The guides who directed us through the vast buildings informed us that no hospital at that time in America even began to be so magnificent. I knew the cost must have been staggering.

While the wards boasted the very latest in equipment, the power and refrigeration plants also were impressive, having the capacity to keep meat for six months to provide against famine or interruption of rail service. Someone gave me a piece of steamed Chinese bread, which looked like raw dough the size of a cupcake. It tasted good, quite like a biscuit.

The hospital's finest private rooms, beautifully furnished, cost patients $5 a day, gold. Even bathing and barber facilities were available.

Though they held a visitors' reception in a large lobby, I refrained from going down the line, having always been averse to shaking hands with people merely for the sake of being able to say I had done it.

At 6:30 I handed my red card to the traffic police, and as our numbers were relayed down the line, it wasn't long before our rickshaws came up. We rode to the station to wait for the train, which, though it looked like an American one outside, was dingy and poorly lighted inside with baggage strewn about.

To me it seemed the funniest thing in the world the way folks traveled out here. Besides trunks, suitcases, and other civilized belongings, they were always followed by boxes of various sizes and shapes, a few rolls done up with straps, a variety of baskets—open and closed, and even vegetables tied up in cloth. I learned that a Chinese gentleman always traveled with a fan in hand, and perhaps a silly-looking little parcel or bag. An American would stick such things in his pockets, but here they seemed to know little of such conveniences.

On the way home, our rickshaw boys started to run like the wind, and we couldn't imagine what occasioned such a burst of speed. But they had merely sighted others in our party ahead and wanted to catch up. We paid our boys for the time, from 3:30 to 8:30 p.m., 75 coppers, or about 50 cents. It had cost just $1.20 to have my trunks and suitcase brought up from the station by hand-pulled cart!

CHAPTER 6

CHINESE AS SHE IS SPOKE

How would you like to visit a Chinese language school with me? Three of us attend daily from the mission in Peking, and we would be tickled to have you come along. First, let me introduce you to my congenial family—Miss Richards, who served later with me in Paotingfu, and Miss Gould—two lovely nurses who lived with me.

It is a bright, crispy morning and we feel like a million dollars, delighted at the chance for a hike. The Chinese, who are not famous walkers, cannot quite understand why we insist on walking when we might take rickshaws. School is just two miles down a broad, hard dirt street, much more pleasant for walking than stone pavement.

Across the street from the American Board Mission stand one story gray stone Chinese buildings. Fortunately, an English sign marks their location, so we know we have arrived. Various classrooms are arranged about several courts, across from the gatekeeper's room. Besides these classrooms, there are tiny cubicles just big enough for you and your private tutor.

We assemble this first morning in the large classroom, some 80 of us, green as grass and twice as dense! Without even a preliminary word, a Chinese gentleman attired in foreign clothes takes the platform and begins to speak, slowly and distinctly. He points to himself and says one word, then to us, pronouncing another, then to someone else with yet another. It finally percolates that he is giving us the personal pronouns.

After these have been oft repeated, sounding much like the three syllables of "Juanita," he produces a book while making a new sound, then a pencil and some money. Finally, he repeats to us such intricate sums such as "This is a pencil"; "that is a book"; "I have money"; with appropriate illustrations.

All day long we listen, never saying a word. Every half hour a new teacher takes his place so we won't acquire any individual's peculiarities. Is it dull? Not a bit, for along with this mere handful of words, the instructors are forever doing funny things to make us laugh. We discover the Chinese are gifted actors and their cleverness at getting ideas across makes it fascinating entertainment.

Everyday a few new words are presented to us, without using a single word of English. By means of objects, acting, illustration, and reiteration, we finally get the idea. But for two whole weeks we never speak a syllable!

At the end of that time we divide into classes with private teachers. Each morning, we first sit in a general class and receive new words. The teacher has to keep giving illustrations until we comprehend. Objects seem easy, but abstract ideas tax his ingenuity to the limit. However, being exceedingly clever, he always gets them across. How would you insert simple words like "if," "method," "dependable," "believe," into the heads of foreigners without using a word of their language and, at the same time, keep them laughing and intensely interested?

Following this general class we go to group classes of eight to nine members or to private teachers. In our group class we speak and use the new words and the old as well. Our instructors answer our questions and help us with difficult words.

"Difficult words"—that is written glibly, but oh, the painful reality behind them. Never did I dream there could be so many strange noises my tongue couldn't pronounce! Of course, it isn't absolutely hopeless, for after much practice one does acquire the knack. For instance, try saying a sound halfway between a "v" and a "w"—all this without mentioning tones. At first my ears cannot distinguish them, but they, too, become educated.

Of course, China is on the opposite side of the world, indicating some things should be upside-down. "Toe" in Chinese, refers to your head. "Shoe" is not to wear, but a book. "Shin" isn't that part of your anatomy above your ankle, but your heart. Also, you nearly always say the same thing twice. You "wait one wait" or "look one look." When asking a question you put the affirmative and the negative together. "Want not want?" has the idea, "Do you want this or not?"

One final peculiarity: one word in the same tone may mean any one of 10 to 30 absolutely unrelated things. You must get the whole context or you haven't an idea what word is being used. A single word by itself has no meaning, so one can't be laconic but must sprinkle a great deal of verbiage over the landscape to make one's meaning clear.

In spite of these eccentricities, Chinese is fascinating, musical and expressive. Also, the written characters are condensed pictures of absorbing interest and much more beautiful than our monotonous alphabet.

A short time ago, we missionaries discovered, to our concern, that two of our most gifted and popular head teachers were not believers. That awakened us to the need of intercession, which we were sure God would answer. When we invited some of the teachers for tea, together with some Christian Chinese, we had the opportunity to speak of eternal things.

One pled the excuse of the opposition of his family. We in America cannot realize what it means to step out and endure persecution. In China the family is a closely bound unit, and to be cast off by one's relations is to be forsaken indeed. But if one really catches a vision of the Lord Jesus, even that sacrifice seems small for His sake. It is so worthwhile just to be able to point longing hearts to the One who can perfectly satisfy, and see the miracle of transformed lives brought about through the power of the Holy Spirit.

If any of you feel your lives are not counting for God at home, perhaps He will allow you to come to China or some other foreign country. It is the greatest privilege in all the world. Who knows, perhaps you will even have the joy of learning the language as I did.

CHAPTER 7

VISITING THE PRESIDENT

On the tenth day of the tenth month, China celebrated the tenth anniversary of the Republic. Shortly after, to my delight, His Excellency, President Hsu Shih Ch'ang, invited the students of the North China Language School to a reception at the presidential residence. This missionary received one of the thrills that come but once in a lifetime, although being an ambassador of the King of Kings is no mean position.

The president's home and its extensive grounds lay within the Imperial City. It is immediately west of the Forbidden City, whose grim walls were crowned with brilliant yellow tile—the same golden glory which roofed all buildings within its limits.

Riding down the broad avenue leading to the president's gate we passed through wall after wall. Although more accustomed to Chinese walls by now, I kept thinking that surely each must be the last. Finally we stood before an imposing gate, gorgeous with multicolored tiles, one of China's great art heritages from a gifted antiquity. Opposite the gate I observed a beautiful screen, or wall of tile, which had a strictly utilitarian purpose—to keep evil spirits from entering.

As we waited for our party of 200 strong to assemble, courteous attendants beckoned us to sign our names at a table. Whether for official records or merely our gratification, I never found out.

At last the great door swung open. To my astonishment, we stood on the shore of a pretty little lake, while three stately boats waited to ferry us across. I felt as though we had left the world of sober fact and were adventuring in a land of make-believe.

The boats had slender cabins, with little runways along each side where the boatmen walked, operating long poles. All too soon we arrived at a white marble landing pavilion.

A few steps brought fairyland for sure, as we saw huge flat rocks piled helter-skelter with enticing caves and winding paths. Climbing up the pile like school children, we noticed to our delight that even the pebbles beneath our feet intertwined in pleasing designs. At the top a grove of sturdy pines bordered a deep mysterious pool. Could the royal children have played here? I wondered.

Rambling down the other side we entered a roofed promenade, its underside adorned with beautiful paintings. What could that fascinating structure ahead be? Probably the only one of its kind in the world; I doubted if the English language had a proper name for it. It appeared to be a roofed-over walk of white marble which actually turned and doubled back on itself, working out an intricate pattern, a thing of delight to the eye. I wished I could run along its turns and twists to trace out the figure and see where it led. At the sides ran a deep granite-lined moat for water lilies and lotus plants.

The nameless structure finally brought us to a stream bordered with graceful gray stone birds and a gray brick building, evidently the presidential residence, surrounded by another moat. Winding through more gates we entered a Chinese building furnished only with large blue upholstered chairs, then passed across a court into the great reception hall built by the old Empress Dowager to entertain foreign guests. It is a sad commentary that the imperial lady built the hall because she felt enraged at her foreign guests' lack of breeding in examining her silks and embroideries when she received them in her own apartments. If they didn't know good manners, she would receive them in the kind of place they were used to! So she roofed over a large court surrounded by four Chinese buildings, using the latter for the walls.

The reception room appeared to be little different from any other. Adorned with a foreign carpet, it stood empty except for a few rows of chairs at either end. I could only wistfully imagine what the original tour might have been like.

We waited on one side in front of the steps by which the president was to enter, before a huge yellow rug of silk velvet portraying two gorgeous dragons battling for the traditional ball of fire.

First, several Chinese secretaries in formal Western dress received us. Then the arrival of a squad of officers announced the president's approach, and formed an avenue down the steps, while we arranged ourselves in a semi-circle in front.

Finally he appeared, descending the steps with a brisk, firm tread, and stood in the center of the yellow rug. Tall and heavyset, his appearance was striking. His face had lines of strength, with a determined chin, piercing eyes, and a high forehead with iron gray hair combed severely back. From the corners of his mouth drooped a gray mustache. In all the assembly, he alone wore Chinese dress, a long garment of brilliant satin with a shorter jacket of blue.

Then, in accordance with state ceremony, he bowed to us three times and we responded in turn, feeling stiff and awkward. This safely accomplished, the president read a brief message of greeting, expressing hope for the continued growth of the language school and expressing appreciation of its service in breaking down barriers to understanding and international friendship. A secretary translated the message in Wen Li, the formal official Chinese language, which even our advanced students could not understand. After a fitting response from the first secretary of the American legation, also a school trustee, His Excellency bowed and departed, followed by his military escort.

After that we were served refreshments of foreign tea and French pastry, following which came an invitation to view the living quarters of the late Empress Dowager. We found them to be pleasant foreign-style rooms, also with blue upholstered furniture.

In an adjacent room we found the bedroom of Her Imperial Highness. To my disappointment, it looked severely plain and simple. At one end stood the "k'ang," made up as for daytime. Though usually of brick, this one consisted all of wood—a sort of platform across the end of the room, used in China as a bed. In its center stood a low redwood table and blue silk pads, on which the Empress sat while working or drinking tea. A narrow bench of redwood served as a step when she climbed down, while two small square tables and a couple of chairs completed the furnishings. Surely little here attested to the voluptuous luxury our Western minds attributed to royalty.

We also viewed the Empress's library which contained no books, but where a stone picture of marvelous beauty held us spellbound.

By now I found myself impressed with two definite features of Chinese architecture: first, the endless succession of walls within walls. Secondly, the buildings themselves were fairly small one-story structures with graceful roofs, built around the four sides of countless stone-paved courts.

Though the gate led us out to a public thoroughfare, our rickshaw boys, to my relief, awaited us. So returning from fairyland, with its dim and dusty past, we stepped back into the workaday world, more convinced than ever that our most worthwhile task ever would be to bring this great land with its noble history the one thing she lacked—the Lord Jesus Christ.

CHAPTER 8

MY FIRST MISSIONARYING
OR
CHANCE ENCOUNTERS OF THE BEST KIND

Friends, Romans, countrymen: lend me your ears! I have just returned from my first country trip, my first touch of honest-to-goodness missionarying, telling of Christ to folks who have never heard His name before. I am so full of the wonder of it, there's apt to be an explosion if I don't bubble over.

Imagine the flutterings as I started for the station and my first railway trip alone in this great China, depending only on my masterful(?) grasp of the language to get me where I wanted to go. (Of course, that would have been like leaning on a broken reed had I not the presence of One who is all-dependable.) It may sound easy, but just think of managing the rickshaw men, porters, getting one's ticket, finding a place for oneself—plus one's belongings—in a crowded car, and all in Chinese! It gave me quite a thrill to be able to do it.

Thoroughly China-ized by this time, I traveled third class with the rest of the population. Railroad service was good, though the palace cars were not so palatial as those in the States. Seats were narrow wooden ones, having a generous rack above to deposit things such as blankets, bundles or bedding rolls. For this trip I contented myself with a "Korie," a sort of straw valise whose capacity is quite elastic.

Though the "chiao hang," or porter, assured me I could find no room in third class, fortunately I discovered a single seat I could have to myself and was quite comfortable. I was thankful for the ancient *Saturday Evening Post* in which I could bury my nose and appear oblivious to the scrutiny, kindly withal, to which foreigners were constantly subjected. One need not parade in the latest Paris creation to be the Mecca of all eyes in China; being foreign was sufficient.

My destination was my "own" Paotingfu, where later I would be assigned permanently. I was to accompany Miss Gumbrell, a delightful fellow-worker, on one of her trips. After being met at the station, I was escorted on foot to our beautiful big compound outside the city wall, not far from the depot. The compound, surrounded by a high wall, a la Chinese style, contained the hospitals, schools, church, and residences.

Spring had arrived, so I was taken around to view the baby goats, newly-hatched chicks, and promising gardens boasted by enterprising housekeepers. Undramatic as it may seem, one must still eat and drink even in China, so gardens and such are essential.

The very next day we donned Chinese clothes and started out. In the country we wore the universal long trousers, with a skirt over them, following the fashion of young China, then a Chinese blouse or long garment. We set off on a freight train, sitting on our luggage.

"An Hsu!" The train groaned and creaked to a halt and two missionaries hopped off, followed by a collection of baggage that would excite many a curious stare in the good old U.S.A., but was quite acceptable in China. A sturdy boy hoisted our Victrola in its blue cloth case to his shoulder, and we set off on foot through fields of gowlian, corn, and cotton for the county seat a mile ahead.

Inside the North Gate we ascended steep stone steps and entered a door bearing the happy legend, "Good News Hall." Through a bare room with rough brick floor and paper windows, we entered first an open court, then, through a side gate, a smaller court and finally a room 10 by 12 feet—our home while in An Hsu.

At the front gate, a Mrs. Chang greeted us with smiles and bows, her wrinkled face radiating peace and joy. Also we meet the pretty young wife of the teacher of the boys' school, Mrs. Feng, and the handsome four-year-old son and heir, Fu Te.

With the help of these good friends, we got our army cots set up, the beds made, and arrangements for our simple housekeeping completed. Using boiling water from the street and some kerosene, potatoes were boiled to eat with chicken carried from home, and we partook of a satisfying meal. Though the worst of the cholera season was over, to avoid risk we refrained from eating Chinese food.

Preliminaries over, a Mrs. Yuan led us out to call. We left the main street quickly to avoid curious stares of loiterers in the shops. Through open gateways we could see workers tying great stocks of gowlian, 10 or 15 feet long, in bundles for the year's fuel supply.

At the first gate we inquired if the grandmother was home and if the dog bit. Assured affirmatively in one case and negatively in the other, we were led in. We found young and old, men and women, busily pulling husks from full ears of yellow corn. At the sight of us they all jumped up—despite our entreaties for them to continue working—and ran to bring out benches to visit and listen. Since they were working against time to get crops in out of the weather, we refused their invitations and stayed but a few minutes, reminding them of the Sunday service. The old grandmother was a baptized believer.

At another gate we were ushered into what appeared to be the office of the head of the family. After seating us on the k'ang, the old gentlemen stood while women folk and children crowded in to hear. This was plainly an upper class family, all being well dressed. Though the former pupil we had come to see turned out not to be of this family, we seized the splendid opportunity to preach the gospel, after the usual polite questions: "How old are you?" "Where do you come from?" "How many are there in your family at home?" "Can you understand our talk?" "How is your hair combed in back?"

All agreed that the good news was truly very good. Who wouldn't believe? They would come to the chapel service the next day. They urged us to stay and escorted us clear to the street, but they didn't come to the service.

Near the chapel an old lady nearly eighty received us with genuine affection. Though she says she trusts the Lord Jesus, she will not give up her old ways. She is a medicine woman and devil worshiper, with elaborate idols before which she continually burns great bunches of incense and kowtows. Our hearts ached as we left this one who had served Satan so long she seemed unable to break his yoke.

Early Sunday morning an old countryman with grizzled head and ragged clothing came in, bringing two small bronze idols. As a token of faith he wanted to give away the images that for generations had been worshiped in his family. Now he had the Truth in his heart instead.

At one home in Ku Ch'ng, a rambling agricultural town, we saw a sweet, forlorn little girl of 11 whose mother had died. The father had a shop on the main street where he lived, so the child lived with an old uncle. Since the uncle was out in the fields from morning till night, she had to stay in utter loneliness to watch the house. Chinese homes are not built to withstand marauders. Even if the door had a lock, the paper windows offered little resistance, so someone was always at home to watch. But one's heart ached when it was a woebegone morsel of 11-year-old girlhood. If only we could find some solution that would permit her to go to school, I thought, not knowing then that one day a solution would be found and the Lord would permit me to have a part in it.

At the next home, old Mrs. Li came out to protect us from attack by the vicious dog. Her husband had been a warm-hearted believer who, when dying, had heard celestial choirs singing of the glory of the Lamb. Tears streamed down her face as she told of the persecution suffered by her daughter married into a heathen family before the family became Christians. As we gently pointed her to the One who can even melt the hatred of a mother-in-law's heart, she dropped to her knees on the cold bricks, joining in prayer for her loved ones.

So it went. Not much fruit for 15 years of mission work, are we tempted to think? But we must remember the town was overrun with shrines and temples; an edifice for idol worship stood at every turn. For hundreds of years these people had known nothing else. While hundreds of temples had known worshipers for centuries, one gospel hall had been open for only a decade. But fear and hatred and misunderstanding were slowly melting away. Now when the foreigner passes by, instead of running to hide, the women hurry out to invite her in. Though the time of seed sowing had been long, surely the harvest was near at hand. But much prayer was needed.

Thus, carrying the little Victrola from America, I had my first opportunity to minister to the two-and-a-half million people for whom the Paotingfu Mission was directly responsible. At present there were only two foreign men and one foreign woman going out into the whole of this vast country field. Do you wonder that this language student is aching to get out?

Florence with Chinese Christian leaders

CHAPTER 9

THE TEMPLE OF HEAVEN

Back in Peking, one morning I heard Dr. Mackey calling excitedly from my doorway. "Guess what?" she caroled. "At last we get to visit the Temple of Heaven everyone has been talking about."

I, too, had been eager to see this much-touted attraction. We learned that to get there we would need to take a rickshaw south through the Tartar City into the Chinese City, going almost to the end, where we would find the gate leading to our destination.

Ah, I thought with satisfaction, again I will have the privilege of seeing what lies behind a Chinese wall.

And so it was. Just before the gates of the Chinese City, we turned in at a red gate in a long wall to our left. Feeling again like a child about to enter a fairyland, I found myself in a wide open space surrounded by great locust trees with gnarled trunks. Walking through this space, we came to another wall where we purchased admission tickets for 30 cents.

Inside, we were enthralled at the sight of an avenue bordered by giant trees. Turning down a delightful woodsy path, we passed through yet another wall. By this time I began to wonder if behind all Chinese walls might be more walls and nothing else.

But no, we finally entered vestibules leading to a court flanked by an imposing building on the right which we approached by marble steps enclosed with marble balustrades. This was the edifice, we discovered, to which the emperor himself came before offering the sacrifice to heaven to purify himself. Adjoining this building stood another court with a structure where the imperial party slept. We peeped into the build-

ing, seeing the camphor wood k'angs, the flat wooden plat-
forms which were their beds. I wondered if they felt as hard as
they looked.

Leaving these buildings, we entered a mysterious forest of
sacred pines to pass through another wall—this time a red one,
with marvelous blue tiles atop it. This wall formed a huge square,
and inside stood huge tubs of brass openwork where incense
had once been offered. Within this square—inside a circular
wall of the same spectacular color—we saw the imposing altar
where the bullock had actually been offered by the emperor for
the propitiation of the people's sins.

In the center of this round enclosure, with the altar on one
side, sat a white marble circular platform, one tier rising above
another. Above this, at the time of the sacrifice, canopies were
erected, we were told, where prayers written on satin were
placed.

The night before the sacrifice, the emperor personally came
to the enclosures where the bullocks for sacrifices were kept to
select an animal without blemish and without spot. As he offered it, slips were tied to it representing the people's sins and
the emperor placed his hands upon the animal's head.

On the marble pavement in front of the temple we stood
on the actual spot where the emperor prayed. As I spoke out
loud there, every word was clearly and uncannily echoed back.
The Chinese called the echo heaven's answer to his prayer.

As we wended our way homeward, I pondered the striking
similarities which convinced early missionaries that China once
had knowledge of the true God. Just as in the Old Testament,
the king actually acted as high priest and mediator, offering
shed blood once each year as propitiation for the sins of the
people. Would this great land come to know Him again, the
Creator of all nations? God alone knew the answer.

Chapter 10

Impressions From Peking

One day about 40 of us received passes to the Forbidden City. Even our rickshaw boys seemed excited to be going, for they simply tore along like mad! When a bunch of them got together, it was a race for them to get ahead of each other.

We entered the gate into the Forbidden City, evidently the part no longer forbidden. At length, pulling up at another wall with a closed gate, we presented our tickets and passed through.

To the left we saw a circular building, a throne hall, dating from about the eleventh century. We crossed a curved white marble bridge over a winding lake. More like a marsh, the lake was filled with reeds and growths. Then before us rose quite a high hill, not wide but steep. As the lake skirted the hill, along with various small temples, we walked for some distance following the hill around. The circular porch was open on the lake side but built up on the hill side, and its ceiling held a mass of paintings, predominantly in bright blue.

Ascending the hill by means of winding stone steps, we came to an oddly-shaped pagoda on top with five sections—base, body, column, ball, and crescent—one above the other, representing the five elements of earth, heaven, fire, air, and ether.

We climbed up several flights of steps of the pagoda. The bottom was white marble, and the upper levels of green and yellow glazed tiles with little Buddha images on each tile. Reaching the highest level to which we could climb, we peered into a small room and saw a fearful-looking Buddha. From this height we could see a beautiful view of the city, and I took a picture of the roofs of the Forbidden City, separated from where we stood by a wide moat and high walls. This "most forbidden part" housed the deposed emperor and the president and government buildings.

Descending by a steep rocky way, we found a cavern running through part of the hill. Crossing another marble bridge, we came to a Buddhist temple not ordinarily open to the public, but by means of the clink of coin we gained admittance. The first building had four dreadful figures on it, and the next, three enormous images of Buddha, flanked by figures of his 18 disciples. The guide told us that the two carved pagoda-like things here were made of mixed copper and gold and were very costly. Because they were dirty and dust-covered, however, they didn't look impressive.

Farther on, the next site of interest was the dragon screen made of tile 50 feet long and 20 feet high. Each series of dragons was in yellow, cream, blue and maroon.

Our tour finally finished, I wanted to see the hostel for the girl students at the mission. Only a 20-minute walk from the language school, it was housed in a Chinese building, formerly the home of a prince and later a provincial governor, and contained 17 courts.

Let me describe this house to you: You enter the gate and find yourself in a small open court paved with stones. To gain entrance through the door in the wall you must step over a high ledge, and you then find yourself in a larger court paved with hard dirt except for stone paths across it. From one-story buildings lining the sides, rooms open out onto the court. Though the court side has a few glass windows, the rest of the walls are paper—that is, a sort of fancy wood latticework, pasted over on the inside with paper which could be easily punched through.

To the right is a passage leading to another court, quite the same, with rooms around it, and so on from passage to court in a great labyrinth. One has to go outdoors across an open court to go from one room to another.

The rooms, now comfortably furnished for the students, each contains a stove. Though paper walls sound airy for cold weather, perhaps they are not.

I was greatly burdened for our schools here. They should be a source of great strength and yet there seemed to be such a leakage. To explain: there were splendid schools at Paotingfu, with almost all the students having a born-again experience, yet the work languished for lack of native leaders. Pitiably few of them entered Christian work. Most of the girls married, scattering over the country. I asked Miss Gumbrell, with whom I was to work in Paotingfu, if the students helped her in her country evangelization, and she said no, she never seemed to run across them, even though the school had been turning out large classes for years. They seemed to be swallowed up, a total loss, so far as the evangelization of China was concerned.

I didn't blame the schools; they may not be at fault. But oh, how I prayed for a quickening from the presence of the Lord that year, that scores of these young people would be touched with a great passion for souls and give their lives to Him unreservedly, and that the Word of the Lord would be glorified throughout the district and bring forth precious fruit.

No way, at that time, could I have known how astonishingly God was to answer that prayer.

CHAPTER 11

ASSIGNED AT LAST

Since language study had been interspersed with delightful trips around that marvelous city of Peking, I had learned to appreciate the history, culture, and life of those wonderful people. But now my first year had ended, and it was time to travel to my first station at Paotingfu, about 100 miles south of Peking, where I would stay at the mission compound.

Our Paotingfu station—containing the men's hospital, the women's hospital, schools for both boys and girls, plus residences for 16 missionaries—had been assigned 12 counties of responsibility. These counties contained 20 million people, and the only missionary working in that area was Miss Gumbrell, the evangelist whom I had been appointed to Paotingfu to assist.

In each of these counties a chapel had been opened and Miss Gumbrell would travel from one chapel to another, holding classes for women and visiting in the homes. As I eagerly joined her on these country trips, I soon found that my language school diction sounded quite different from the jargon the country people spoke, but gradually my ear became attuned so I could understand and they could understand me.

Every day we scarcely would finish supper before our first visitors arrived—girls, big and little, and women, asking after our welfare and later attending the evening service. Many were strangers coming to 'ch'iao ping' (to see the doctor). One by one, we taught them to read, using brightly colored slips—some with a simple prayer and others with a song. A rather free translation of the prayer would be: "I beseech thee, Jesus, to save me, act as my mediator, and forgive my sins and iniquities." The song, which has a fine rhythm in Chinese, speaks of the only one true God, who loves and forgives us, and of Jesus, who gave His life to wash our heart. The people loved it, and from these simple seed thoughts it was easy to enlarge and present quite a bit of truth.

By church time the crowd became too big for the chapel, so Miss Gumbrell took a group of those who had never heard the gospel into another room. In a special service, she explained to them simply and clearly the good news of salvation.

After the service the doctor's work began and we continued to talk to the people as they waited. (I must explain the "we." My discourses were yet brief. The Chinese usually understood me, but frequently floored me with a whirlwind of talk beyond my depth. There were heaps of common words I didn't know yet, while many I did know were quite different here in the country.)

You must wonder what the homes of these common people looked like. Let me describe them: A wall of sun-dried mud bricks can be entered through a gate made of gowlian stalks. The court is larger than those in the city, often with a little garden. Some crude wooden farming implements and half worn-out pots are scattered about. At the sides of the court three or four three-room buildings house the mother-in-law and the sons and their families. Smoke from the middle room, where food is prepared over a low pipeless brick stove, has blackened the walls.

Fully half of the adjoining room is occupied by the k'ang, built of brick or wood and covered by a straw mat. In one corner is the pile of quilts in which the family rolls up at night.

But the women! Always so hospitable and delighted to have us enter their homes, where they listen intently to the Truth. Some are beautiful in the strength of young womanhood, some twisted and bent by the hard, meager years. But to all, the story of God's love, the finished redemption, and the new life in Christ Jesus is good news without question for they know the depths of sin, the horror of hatred and selfishness, the slavery of superstition. Long have they sought peace through a multiplicity of gods, sacrifices, and burning of incense, and found it not. Because of the very blackness of their night the gospel shines with redoubled glory.

If any doubt the power of the gospel, would they might see some of its fruits in China. The wonderful fortitude, the joy and peace, the simple faith and saintly living of those who came to the Lord from the midst of heathenism, have no explanation save the grace of God and a new life in Christ. No social gospel, no culture, no education, no "fanning of the divine spark," is sufficient. Nothing short of God's power in regeneration will do. Can you imagine a more joyful task than meeting such a tremendous need with an altogether sufficient remedy? That was the priceless privilege conferred upon us.

But unbeknownst to me at that time, within a few months after my arrival at the Paotingfu station, I was to experience a great shock, and to find myself alone—the sole missionary evangelist to the millions of Chinese in the great area of Paotingfu. For while my dear friend and fellow worker Miss Gumbrell was visiting in Peking, Dr. Lewis, at Paotingfu, received an urgent telegram: "Come for Miss Gumbrell, immediately." We could not imagine what it meant, but to our sorrow we soon knew the answer.

Chapter 12

A Huge Loss —
and a Momentous Decision

For several hours we walked in the shadow of death, still very much in the dark. Our hearts were sore and eager for any word. Of course the first telegram meant something had happened to Miss Gumbrell and she must be in serious condition. Later came a second telegram, "Operate Gumbrell tonight. Pray." Then still later came a letter written Sunday, telling us that when Miss Gumbrell was returning from the hospital after a fall on Thursday, her rickshaw man had fallen and she, being weak, fell out of the rickshaw over him. We remembered that she had been brought back from the brink of death by prayer years ago, from a helpless paralytic to a robust body, so we knew that if it was for His glory, He would raise her up again.

How can I tell it? Early the next morning came a telegram: "Casket will arrive seven o'clock. Notify country Christians."

That noon a letter from Dr. Mackey explained everything. Miss Gumbrell was operated on Monday evening for acute peritonitis with a perforation. The fall had only hastened matters and possibly saved her from a long period of suffering. She lived a night and day after the operation and gave a glorious testimony to all with her as to what the Lord could do for a Christian passing into the valley of the shadow.

Who can estimate the effect of her homegoing on my life and work? Mrs. Cunningham said to me the next day, "Oh, if you hadn't come!" It appeared that the Lord let Miss Gumbrell remain on earth just long enough for me to get a wee start. Now, how I was cast on the Lord! And the burden for the hundreds of thousands of women and girls for whom I alone was responsible! How could the Lord use such as I? I knew His will and love and purpose are perfect, but how He could take such a valuable servant and leave so worthless a one is past understanding.

Her homegoing must be for His glory. How I prayed it would mean a reviving throughout the country, that hearts of hundreds who had listened indifferently to her preaching would now be turned to the Lord, and that from this life laid down would spring up scores of young Chinese to proclaim the glad news.

I felt this was a time of crisis in my own life, but I was still too stunned to realize what it all meant. I could but continue to pray the Lord would mold me to His use, and that I would not fail Him.

Dr. Lewis thought the fall had nothing to do with Miss Gumbrell's death. The place of her former operation was still perfect; the doctors had never seen anything like it. God had healed her in answer to prayer and given her seven-and-a-half more years of life, whereas no one had ever been known to survive an operation of that kind for more than four or five years. Dr. Lewis said, "I can't see it any other way, than that the Lord gave her these last two years to prepare you for the work."

Her heart was at rest, for she said the Lord had prepared me to take up the work. She had hoped we might have another year together, but since it wasn't His will, she knew it would be all right. It was her desire I should go to live with Dr. Mackey to take Miss Gumbrell's place. Of course she realized nothing could be a greater help to me.

No one can realize how unworthy and helpless all this made me feel. My comeliness was indeed turned to corruption. I remembered Dwight L. Moody once said the Lord was just looking for a man poor and weak and useless enough that He could use and so He picked on him. If those were the qualifications for usefulness, I never felt them more. I came to the place where

I was absolutely without strength. All that was done from this point on would be His doing.

Many things of the last weeks and months now took on new significance. The next Sunday afternoon when I conducted the service I felt led to say that the Lord might be about to lead some of us out into an unknown way, a path where we had not gone before. My theme was that faith could be victorious when it could not understand. But how little did I dream it was me whose feet were to be set on those unknown paths. Later I saw that the Lord was preparing my heart.

Miss Gumbrell had scheduled a women's leader's class to take place in a few weeks. I had to decide whether or not to cancel it. With my uncertain grasp of the language, should I try to teach it? I agonized over the answer. Finally I realized it was a case of sink or swim and I decided to swim, but only after intensive hours of preparation with a language teacher. Every word, every tone, had to be exactly right. And, to my joy, my efforts paid off. How glad I was to have made the decision in prayer! The women seemed delighted. They could understand their new missionary and felt comforted after the loss of their dear friend Miss Gumbrell.

So I carried on with the work in the country much as Miss Gumbrell had done. North China is most conservative. The word for wife is "inner person." She is the one who dwells in the inner court and is never seen in public. So as we journeyed about visiting in homes, we were careful never to travel on the big street but, rather, to strip through alleys and back lanes and use side doors so we would not offend people by seeming brazen in showing ourselves on the main streets.

I say "we" because a Chinese Bible woman and a helper always accompanied me. Sometimes one of the women doctors went along to hold clinics and we could talk to the patients as they waited to be seen. This being an effective method in reaching the Chinese, we saw no reason to change it. But the day would come, not many years distant, when the Lord Himself would change it, opening up new approaches to evangelism that I—young, new on the field, and inexperienced—could only dream about.

CHAPTER 13

A FAMILY PICTURE

The charm of the new and unexpected was the constant traveling companion of the itinerator in China. Thus with anticipation I packed up my traps one March morning to visit a solitary family of Christians some 40 li away.

Wouldn't you know it! When the cart arrived and had been filled with my luggage, the driver announced his animal couldn't haul the load. But after a long altercation it appeared the animal might be persuaded if 150 coppers were added to the price earlier agreed upon.

The pugnacious driver, whose disagreeable face matched his disposition, nearly came to blows with everyone he met on the road. About the time I became apprehensive of ever reaching our destination, his fiery temper cooled and we traveled in peace.

About mid-day, we came upon a temple fair, where as far as eye could see the landscape appeared black with human beings, gathered to buy and sell or to acquire virtue by burning incense in the temple. Above the thousands of voices hawking goods, we could hear the sound of clanging cymbals, drums, and the high-pitched singsong of theater performance. It reminded me that China's population is no less than teeming millions.

Finally, across the river, we arrived at the farm home of the Hao family, where young and old protested they had been watching for me for hours. Soon, with my possessions, I became established in a large apartment that would be mine for a week, and began to try to get the family relationship straightened out.

First I met two brothers, men of splendid physique, with strong, frank faces. The elder, a widower, had an only son, a youth of 17. When his mother died a few months before, this lad's long-standing engagement had been consummated so his bride, five years his senior, might keep house for father and son. A sensible, capable girl, she seemed to fit comfortably into the family life.

The younger brother's household was more numerous, over which his wife, a wise, gentle lady, presided harmoniously. Three strapping sons and one small daughter completed their family.

The eldest son, obviously the pride of the family, was a promising young doctor on the men's hospital staff in Paotingfu. But after Chinese fashion, his charming wife had to remain in the old home performing the duties of a good daughter-in-law.

In China you would never ask if a young woman is a good wife and mother. It was always, "Is she a good daughter-in-law?" By this is meant: Is she submissive and obedient to her husband's mother, respectful and attentive to her wants, strong and clever, able to cook and sew and weave? If these can be answered in the affirmative, and in due time she presents her mother-in-law with grandsons, she has honorably discharged her marriage obligation and will doubtless live to be honored and served in turn by her sons' wives. In most cases, it was not the husband but the mother-in-law who made or marred a married woman's happiness.

The second son, the stay-at-home farmer, helped his father cultivate the ancestral acres. His wife, a dainty, graceful girl, exemplified perfectly the Chinese classical requirements for beauty—a delicate oval face, fair complexion, glossy black hair, slender hands, and tiny bound feet on which she swayed gently as she walked, like a lovely blossom on its stem.

Living arrangements for this large family were comfortable as befitted well-to-do country folk. Facing the door in my room were beautiful tall China vases, arranged on a long sideboard, part of the dowry of every well-set-up maiden. Opposite the k'ang were a set of cupboards and chests: one for the husband and one for the wife. It would be improper for them to use the same one.

After news of the foreigner's arrival visitors soon crowded in. Such opportunities were the joy and the despair of the country preacher. Often the dear old women are tragically deaf, and the young ones usually nursing fretful babies, plus shoals of bright-eyed kiddies. Practically all were hugely interested in the foreigner's shoes and the way she combed her hair. Sometimes the heterogeneous crowd gave attention; sometimes one spoke against great odds. It was discouraging when each soul did not quaff at once the "water of life," but encouraging that sometimes the Spirit caused a thirst in the most unlikely circumstances. The Word that is "quick and powerful" is never sent forth in vain.

Each night quite a group gathered for family prayers. One evening I felt led to teach practically on Ephesians five and six, dwelling on the family as the Lord meant it to be in the wondrous relationship between husband and wife. I noticed everyone seemed particularly interested. After I retired, the family, in an adjoining room, talked on into the small hours of the morning. It was not until the next day I learned why. It seemed the dainty little wife of the farmer son held her husband in contempt, causing a great blot on the family happiness. Last evening's lesson had touched the sore spot, and they spent half the night lovingly trying to bring the lessons home to the erring wife. So many kinds of heartaches, but the Word has healing for them all.

Sunday, after preparing for the morning service, I joined the women in a holiday pastime—making chu poa poas. A spoonful of finely chopped cabbage and pork is enclosed in a thin flour and water paste, then these little dumplings are arranged on great circular trays. Everyone helps and has as much fun as an American family over a taffy pull. Though I usually prepared my own meals in the country, I gladly accepted an invitation to join the family. The women folk sat on the k'ang with great bowls of steaming chu poa poas within easy reach, while the men sat at a table similarly supplied. With bowls and chopsticks, we enjoyed a royal feast.

The noon meal over, a continuous congregation sat until dark, testing the preacher's ingenuity and endurance, but she was glad to present the truth over and over in a hundred different forms. When the meeting dispersed, it was after ten o'clock and I thought gratefully of my army cot, feeling I had completed a full day. But as I went to the gate with our women guests, a crowd of men came in, seating themselves on the just-vacated benches.

They introduced me. One was the village school teacher, held in high esteem. I felt puzzled as to the reason for their call. Conversation languished, and everyone seemed to be waiting for something. Finally in an aside to Mrs. Hao, I inquired if they expected me to preach to them.

"They have come to listen," she gently replied.

Such an audience was not of my choosing; my work was normally with women and children. But God answered a hasty prayer for help, and a message came from the Book somewhat suited to their condition and intelligence.

We parted with mutual love and respect which made us regret the necessity of parting. It was not until later that a spasm of anti-foreign feeling across the country caused much disillusionment and pain. But at that time, race did not matter for we knew we were of one family.

CHAPTER 14

FUNERAL OF MADAME FENG YU HSIANG

Startlingly varied have been the sights the grim gray walls of Paotingfu have looked down upon in the past two decades. Nowhere in history has a country been catapulted along with China's amazing speed, and no people in a single generation have changed so radically the entire aspect of their thoughts and purposes.

These walls witnessed the madness of 1900, the wild fanaticism which plunged the land into the coils of the very international relationships she sought to avoid. The blood of martyrs—poured out within their ken, by some magic more powerful than the incantation of the Boxers—became living tentacles binding the hated foreigners to the very soil that tried to expel them forever.

Thereafter, change strode with seven league boots through the country torn so rudely from her exclusivism. In 1911 these walls also watched the burning, looting, and killing of the terrible revolution days. But this radical political revolution is less marvelous than the revolution in thought that has been working ever since—the complete new system of education, renaissance in literature, and the seething turbulence of new social, political, and philosophical thinking.

With this background in mind, you may catch the significance of the unusual service which took place under the shadow of these same walls on December 18, 1923.

It was the funeral of the wife (and in China it is meaningful to say "only" wife) of Feng Yu Hsiang, known throughout the world as the "Christian" general.

Almost the whole Christian community awaited the funeral train, bringing 500 soldiers as well as official representatives from the capital. After greeting the foreign friends, the general quickly struck off on foot down the railroad track to the burying ground. He obviously wanted to avoid the painful prolonged meetings with those who had gathered to offer condolences. So rapidly did his long stride carry him, he was a hundred yards away before his bodyguards sprinted after their idolized commander.

The family cemetery lay on the site of General Feng's boyhood home, where a year before he had placed his parents' remains with true filial piety. Over the grave had been erected a matting structure. Here the general awaited the arrival of the catafalque in which the casket was borne from the station. When he learned the missionaries had come, he invited them into the matting pavilion where they were courteously seated and served tea.

Soon strains of music announced the procession. First came the local police band in blue uniforms and gold epaulets, a military band from Peking, and, in between, scores of artificial wreaths of exquisite workmanship. Mourners in white—one son, two daughters, nephews and nieces—immediately proceeded the catafalque.

A company of heathen women began wailing hysterically as they entered the pavilion, but were speedily quieted with the admonition that that wasn't part of a Christian funeral. Though Mrs. Feng was for many years a baptized Christian, most of her family and some of the general's relatives were unbelievers. These had prepared a table of food and, before the Christian service, were given an opportunity to light candles and bow, their customary way to show respect for the dead. However, Pastor Liu, who conducted the service, explained that this also was not part of the Christian rites.

The service was simple: a hymn, "Safe In The Arms Of Jesus," was sung by the high school girls, followed by the reading of the burial service and prayer. Then as soldiers filled the trench, the Christians sang glad hymns of the home beyond. On the heaped- up mound lay a few wreaths of fresh white chrysanthemums and a white cross.

Why this elaborate description? Because the man who wished to glorify the Lord in every detail of his wife's funeral had been a young soldier in a group of curious onlookers who heard Miss Morrill (called the "holy woman") plead with the Boxers for the lives of the Chinese Christians. That incident set his heart hungering after the Truth. Today, by the grace of God, he was perhaps the outstanding figure among four hundred million for his courageous war on vice and luxury, his fidelity and care for his soldiers, and his splendid system of vocational training, giving glory to the Lord whom he preached by word as well as his life.

Even the men of his far-famed "Christian Army" were different. They possessed that indefinable something belonging to twice-born men; their devotion, discipline, and courtesy in marked contrast to the usual Chinese soldiery.

A soldier expressed the attitude of his men: "It isn't easy to be a soldier for Feng Yu Hsiang, but we know he loves us!" Each one of the general's men was required to learn to read and write and learn a trade so he would be independent when he left the ranks, instead of a brigand as was usually the case. They became masons, carpenters, makers of bamboo chairs, tailors, blacksmiths, shoemakers, and so on. When a man left the army, he received a kit of tools for his trade and sometimes a position was found for him as well.

General Feng put his finger on the sore place in our school system when he said we ought not to take poor boys into a beautiful foreign school and educate them to be unfit to go back into their homes and support themselves.

Of course I was young and green and not a school teacher, so had no right to speak, but I wondered if we had not made a vast blunder in taking a cumbersome educational system developed to fit the needs of Western civilization, transporting it bodily to a land where antecedents and conditions are as different as day and night. Though schools here have done much good, it seemed a Chinese system could be developed that would be more efficient.

Our big boy's middle school in Peking was of high grade professionally. But it was heartbreaking to hear how the boys themselves spoke of its spiritual condition. They said it was hard to be a Christian there because of the persecution by the majority who were non-Christians. To evidence interest in the Bible was to be hooted at. I feared we were turning out heathen rascals, a tragic use of consecrated money to maintain such a school. But I knew prayer could change things.

Nearly all the missionaries had educated children, and the results had frequently been far from satisfying. But it seemed I would rather provide schools fitted to the students' circumstances where they could support themselves if need be. The initiative and self-dependence developed would be a great asset.

Were these dangerous sentiments I was expressing? I didn't know. Perhaps in the future God would open doors for a new kind of school. Hopefully, I would be wiser as opportunity came for further observation.

CHAPTER 15

THE CHINESE FAMILY SYSTEM

The Chinese family system is strong. So much so, that one day Mr. Yang, the progressive youth who was one of my language teachers while I was there as a missionary, said, "My father and mother are going to let my wife come here to go to school." This, spoken in English, sounded strange indeed.

Engagements in many cities were still made by parents, usually when children were very young. These were most binding. In fact, a wedding invitation I received to the marriage of one of our schoolteachers, issued by the groom, said that in accordance with the engagement made by his deceased father, he would celebrate his marriage on a certain day.

When asking if a girl is engaged, one asked if she has a mother-in-law. That showed the significant part of Chinese marriages, as the husband was rather incidental. It was the mother-in-law who made life for the bride, and usually she made it exceedingly miserable indeed. Though at the time of the wedding a room was prepared or a new building built for the bride, she was nothing more than a servant, sometimes a much abused one, until she presented her mother-in-law with a grandson. Then she assumed a more respected position; however, she remained absolutely under the thumb of the mother-in-law as long as the latter lived.

Finally comes the time of her supremacy when she herself becomes a mother-in-law and can seemingly take revenge for all her own mistreatment by making her daughter-in-law suffer. Although the place of the woman was supposed to be inferior to that of the man, in the home the mother-in-law usually ruled the roost. It was a son's duty to take a wife to serve his mother and provide children to carry on the family name. He himself might even be away from home year in and year out, but his wife stayed home with his mother.

This system did have its advantages however, for in a large family, each person was mutually interdependent, and it was almost unknown for one to strike out independently on his own. How different this culture was to what I had been accustomed to in the States.

CHAPTER 16

THOSE IN AUTHORITY
(A BIT OF LEVITY, NOT TO BE MISCONSTRUED)

I believe the idea is current in some circles that missionaries between furloughs are sort of embalmed. When they return to their homeland, they emerge from their camphor and mothballs for a brief contact with life. Then, upon going back to the mission field, they slip back into a coma-like existence for another period.

This out-of-the-world idea may sound well but it didn't come within hailing distance of the facts (or else someone I knew hadn't yet awakened to her mummified condition!).

Now there is low life and high life. Without laying claim to a steady diet of the latter, I aver that even in interior China we sometimes burst out on an elevated level. Personally I could not boast of being chummy with the great ones on earth, but could modestly announce in the social columns that we entertained at dinner a man who was one of the greatest powers in the Republic, governor of our province, and seriously advocated for president— Marshall T'sao K'un. We were equally honored on the same occasion with the presence of the diplomatic representative of our own great land, the American minister Dr. Jacob Gould Schurman, for many years president of Cornell University. With these two distinguished visitors came a host of stars of lesser magnitude, any one of whom would have been quite thrilling by himself.

Now this juicy plum fell into our laps without so much as a shake of the tree. It happened this way:

An American in Manchuria got himself shot by a Chinese guard and very carelessly died as a result, leaving no end of international complications. In the course of negotiations on the subject it became necessary for the American minister to interview the powers behind the throne. Advantage being taken of an opportune invitation, the minister and his suite arrived, ostensibly to see the historic Paotingfu mission station, but practically on a diplomatic errand to T'sao K'un.

Being merely women in China, the feminine portion of our compound family had no part in the early affairs of the day. The men met the special train which brought the visitors from Peking at noon. The whole party went directly to the governor's park where they were feasted with foreign food before the conferences begun.

At six-thirty all were to be our dinner guests. We prepared accordingly, three long tables in the finest house on the compound, with dishes and silver and linen borrowed indiscriminately. In common courtesy, an invitation was extended to the governor and his staff, though no one was so bold as to believe the busy man of affairs would accept. He would send his foreign secretary to represent him, the usual and expected procedure.

Supper time came. The foreign guests, including our friends of the American Board mission in the south suburb, arrived. We chatted informally—the minister was a man with whom it was easy to converse, and soon some of the Chinese guests came in.

But then the stupendous rumor was noised about that the governor himself was coming! There was a hurried rearranging of place cards and the setting of another plate. The matter of precedence in seating guests is a serious and complicated matter in China. I'm sure we shattered every rule, for in our blunt American practicality we were solely concerned with getting the places so arranged that there would be a fluent linguist to act as conversation pivot between the Chinese-speaking and English-speaking guests. Of course our most accomplished scholar served as connecting link for the governor and the minister.

At last he arrived, dressed in a foreign-style business suit. When introduced, I didn't quite know whether to bow a la Chinese or shake hands a la American. I chose the bow as being safest. Then everyone found their places, grace was said, and dinner started.

There followed a sleight-of-hand performance unnoticed by the guests in general, which almost convulsed those of us who were "on the inside."

Two of our menfolks had places at the end of the third table near the door. They were just seated when Mr. Stevenson noticed two more guests arriving—the chief of police and another official. Someone had invited them, but no one knew they were coming. Springing to his feet, Mr. Stevenson welcomed them with one hand, while with the other he nudged his companion. The latter also rose and with effusive courtesy the latecomers were installed in the seats just vacated. So smoothly was it done that scarcely a soul knew anything had happened.

So far so good. The soup had just been removed when the Tao Yin, or district magistrate, arrived, likewise unexpectedly. Mrs. Stevenson, as hostess, went forward, greeted him graciously and ushered him back to her own seat, where fortunately the next course had not yet been served. This again was done without attracting the least attention and neither did the Tao Yin dream that his place had not been waiting for him!

In the course of the talk at table the governor mentioned some ornamental stonework in which he was specializing, and asked Dr. Lewis what he would like for beautifying his hospital. The medico replied that he wasn't very particular about rocks; he was more interested in rooms and beds for the sick people he had to turn away for lack of space.

The governor laughed, and two days later his financial secretary called the doctor to the yamen to promise $20,000 for a new dispensary.

I don't remember much about the dinner itself. It might have boasted a more elaborate menu, but we didn't wish to give a wrong impression. It was sadly true that sometimes non-missionary visitors were treated to the finest dainties the country could afford as a special recognition and honor. Then they returned home and dilated on the luxurious way the missionaries lived. They did not realize that what they had enjoyed was not an ordinary meal, but all the precious tidbits saved many months for such a festive occasion.

At the conclusion the governor spoke briefly on the friendship of America and China. His remarks in Wen Li (the classical language) were translated into English by his foreign secretary, a young Chinese educated in America.

At nearly eight o'clock, the hour set for the return of the minister's special to Peking, the party broke up with a mighty bustle of cranking and tooting in the front yard, where were parked about all the motor vehicles the city could boast—from the lavender limousine of the governor to the Fords of lesser dignitaries. Feeling very metropolitan, we could almost fancy ourselves on Broadway or Michigan Boulevard.

What did it all signify? It meant, at least, a degree of friendliness toward missionaries and their cause. On our side, it meant a better appreciation of those in authority, and a determination to pray more faithfully for them. And truly there seemed to be small hope for China nationally until her official classes had experienced a change of heart.

CHAPTER 17

WASHED-OUT ROADS AND BALKY MULES

Much as Miss Gumbrell had been doing, I went on with work in the country. Sometimes we were remarkably led, as in the exciting trip home from Lai Yuen. Scheduled to move on to T'ang An Yi, we heard the swollen rivers were impassable, so inquired as to the possibility of getting back to Paotingfu. On Saturday, we hired pack mules, setting Tuesday as the departure date.

Between our eagerness to get home and fear that another rainy spell would hinder us, we felt in a furor. Then on Sunday noon a man suddenly arrived from T'ang An Yi to take us there for a long anticipated visit.

"You have no idea how many people expect you," he urged. "We posted announcements to advertise the clinic, and when the rain began, one old lady called her daughter home just to pray that the river wouldn't rise so you will get there!"

My heart touched, I told Deacon Lien we would go for a week. But it seemed hardly possible to get our belongings across the swift river, 100 feet wide and 4 feet deep.

Tuesday morning found us packed; though the sky appeared dull gray and it sprinkled, heavy rain did not appear imminent.

As we waited for the mules to arrive, several men left with picks and shovels to mend the trail. They returned with news that our delay had been of the Lord; had we started, we could not have gotten through because of serious washouts just repaired that day.

With this evidence of God's care, we started out happily the next morning at six o'clock, reaching an inn for lunch. To our dismay, we discovered that in those six hours we had covered only eight miles. I'm sure they had to be the longest miles in the country, as we had to walk nearly all the way up and down two mountain ranges.

In the afternoon our animals forded one creek after another. That night, at another inn, I realized I had never before ached in quite so many places at one time. After a long weary night, starting out the next morning proved a relief. Fortunately, we fell in with a train of experienced mule drivers who knew the way perfectly, especially since we had to cross 15 large rivers. Choosing the wrong fording place could have been serious.

Now we found ourselves part of a train of some 50 pack animals bound for Paotingfu. Some of the drivers seemed careless, accounting for two accidents we witnessed. In one place three animals nearly buried themselves in a mud hole, taking a gang of men and much time to extricate them. Mules seem to have a fondness for walking along the extreme edge of a cliff. This was always a trial to me, but I wasn't able to change their habits. When heavy rain made everything soft this was particularly dangerous.

I meditated this as we followed along a stretch that looked unsafe. Suddenly there was a commotion ahead: the cliff edge had given way and a mule went sprawling with a great clatter 20 feet down to the rocky river bed below. I supposed that the animal had been killed, but neither he nor his pack were injured.

That evening we stopped at a nice inn in a prosperous village surrounded by beautiful orchards. All night and the next morning it poured, so we had no hope of getting home that day. Since the inn proved to be clean and quiet, we slept most of the day, making up much lost rest.

In the afternoon the rain stopped, but when we looked at the sky, it was most unpromising, with clouds, blacker and yet blacker, rolling in. We wondered if we were doomed for an indefinite stay.

As a few drops fell and we started back to the inn, an old lady intercepted us, begging us to come into her yard and visit. A crowd of well-dressed women and children had gathered.

"You are guests," the old lady told us, "and we will be glad to make your acquaintance."

What more could an evangelist want? When I told her we had come to preach the "Jesus way," she insisted on procuring benches so all could sit down and listen. The old woman grasped the truth in a marvelous way and eagerly took the initiative in learning a little prayer.

When we rose to leave, I noticed the sky had suddenly cleared. It was forced upon me that there was a connection between my talk with the elderly lady and the passing of the clouds. I wonder if the Lord had kept us there just long enough for that eager soul to have a chance to learn of the Way of Life!

Before four a.m. we were on our way, though washed-out roads made hard going by moonlight. It was so muddy I could get no relief by walking, but we were homeward bound and felt neither heat nor weariness, hunger nor thirst. Several times we had narrow escapes. Miss Chao's mule jumped a ditch and nearly threw off both pack and rider. Also, Mrs. Li's mule started through a passage so narrow he must inevitably leave his load behind. He was hauled back just in time.

My mule was a mystery. The driver, insisting that the animal had a very bad disposition, led him faithfully almost every step of the way. I expected any moment he would display some bad trick, but we reached home without a single bit of conduct to bear out his unsavory reputation.

CHAPTER 18

1925: UNREST BEGINS

When national hero and Chinese statesman Sun Yatsen died, things changed. First, Peking Union Medical school had to close without examinations or graduates. Representatives arrived from Peking to stir up the students in Paotingfu. Even two nurses' training schools received inflammatory letters from Peking that read, "If anyone ought to be angry against the foreigners, it is the nurses!" Our school girls, cared for carefully and not allowed on the street without a teacher, now rushed out daily to harangue listeners.

One afternoon our kitchen staff received a student cartoon, presenting a hawk and a lion tearing a Chinaman to pieces. "Ha ha, we'll eat him up!" read the caption. The hawk was labeled England and the lion Japan.

The next morning excitement prevailed at the girls' school. A girl had jumped in the well! Since that was a favorite way here to die for your country, it seemed connected with the political turmoil. Later that day it came out she did it to spite her teacher, who was investigating a case of theft. The girl came from Tsang T'sun. I was much ashamed of her.

After this event, we felt it wise not to venture out unless necessary, especially on the train or street. Even some of the most sane and loyal people were fearfully worked up.

"At the Boxer time," Dr. Mackey stated, "one felt one's enemies were those on the outside, but now our own children we raised have turned against us."

Riots and killings occurring in Hankow make me feel as though I were sitting on the edge of a crater and anything might start things off. I secretly found myself longing to be taken across the Pacific on a U.S. cruiser to safety.

The worst was against the British, and poor Miss McKillican dared not venture out on the street. It seemed comical when she was a gentle English soul who had given a lifetime for China.

At church Mr. Wang preached an inflammatory sermon against England. So many terrible conditions existed here: brigandage, civil war, famine, with a toll of lives and suffering, and the people accepted it without turning a hair. But one little collision with a foreign power and the whole country burst into flames!

Our mission shelter was adequate for any emergency, but we had no assurance that one would not arise. Some thought there was nothing to the political situation but others believed a massacre was imminent.

Mr. Waller, the British Salvation Army man, was practically driven out of town. He couldn't get a rickshaw to carry him or coolies to do anything for him. The British chapel at Taiyuanfu was attacked by a mob and the missionary in charge injured. It was sad when so many British lives had been laid down for China. "This is the first time I have ever felt the Chinese don't want us," Dr. Mackey said sadly.

Always before people laughed when the Consul ordered them out. But this time everyone was glad to obey. If we left, we would be eager to see how the Chinese rose to the responsibility of the work. It would mean more for the development of the church than we could accomplish in many years. I felt grateful for my tiny four years here, grateful for every dirty little hut in the out-of-the-way places where I had the privilege of telling the glad story.

Chapter 19

Thumbnail Sketches

In those days when the Chinese situation was so hard to understand, I wished everyone could know personally some of my dear friends. We shared many experiences together. Let me relate some of them to you.

Mrs. Chang

Mrs. Chang was a devoted Christian who lived in the village of Kan Chong. One spring while a station class was in progress she came daily to study at the chapel, a mile from her home. She carried a heavy burden for her relatives, most of whom were much opposed to the gospel.

A young nephew who lived next door suddenly became very ill. The family burned quantities of incense, presented offerings to the idols, and invited in old medicine women who supposedly were able to charm away the evil spirit causing the disease.

Meanwhile Mrs. Chang explained that these means were futile, that only the Lord of heaven could heal. In response to her entreaties they asked her to pray.

"What could I do?" she asked. "While I was in the room praying they were outside burning incense. How could the Lord answer?"

The lad grew worse. Finally Mrs. Chang secured a reluctant consent to invite the missionary doctor, who had been holding clinic at the chapel, to come. She called for the two of us in her ox-drawn cart.

A brief examination proved the patient to be in an advanced state of spinal meningitis. He was as stiff as a board. It would be too difficult to get him to the hospital so the doctor could only leave medicines and directions for making him more comfortable. On the way home she explained carefully to Mrs. Chang that no human power could save the boy's life; only the Lord's miracle working touch could cure him.

Several weeks later we heard the sequel. After our departure the boy became much worse and the next day his family gave him up and ceased even to watch by his bedside. They were very bitter and insisted that the foreign pills had killed him.

Poor Mrs. Chang was in deep trouble. If he died, the animosity of the family toward Christianity would know no bounds. There was only one relief for her burdened heart—her prayers. She knelt on the k'ang beside the prostrate form and poured out her prayer. Not a few minutes, but all night, she stayed and interceded for her nephew. In the morning, the boy's mother objected to hearing this valiant prayer hero, so Mrs. Chang betook herself to her own room and continued her supplication.

By that afternoon the lad was much better and able to take a little nourishment. He continued steadily to improve and in two weeks was running around as bright and active as ever, with none of the sorry aftereffects that so frequently follow that dread disease.

We joined Mrs. Chang in praying that this mighty deliverance would someday win this family to the Great Physician who has power to save eternally.

Mrs. Shih

Mrs. Shih was a woman of humble station and no brilliant gifts, but the reality of her Christian experience had been tested by the years. During the winter I heard that she was in desperate circumstances and sought an interview. She was entirely self-respecting as she appeared in her clean but faded garments. I inquired about her daughter who was sick at home with tuberculosis, and urged the importance of giving her nourishing food.

"Oh," Mrs. Shih said simply, "We can't buy food. We are really starving."

Amid the tragic hopelessness of it there came to me a desperate faith, and we had a long talk about the promises of God to His children. The assurance came to us that He had a way out, and we sought it on our knees. As we arose I asked about a younger sister of Mrs. Shih, a doctor working in the South. She had married during the year and Mrs. Shih did not know her new address.

After a Chinese woman marries she has no claim on her maiden home or her own relatives. She enters the family of her husband and, in theory at least, breaks all other ties. So according to custom it would be exceedingly farfetched to expect any help from a younger sister who was also married. Knowing, however, that the doctor was an earnest Christian and feeling sure she would want to help her unfortunate sister, I suggested to Mrs. Shih that we write to her and pray the Lord to deliver the letter. It was done; the doctor's old address was learned from friends, and we trusted that her mail would be forwarded to her new home.

Meanwhile, on pretext of furnishing dainties for the sick girl, I gave Mrs. Shih money to tide her over until a reply could be expected. The Lord was faithful and sent back the needful relief, so this dear woman had another deliverance to add to the tale of former mercies.

Mr. Wang

When the dread of "rice Christians" is upon one, and one fears lest the church be polluted by the temptation to grasp after material advantage, it was mighty heartening to meet a man like Mr. Wang. Because he was generous to a fault, some people whispered that he was a bit "off." For my part, I only wished that every Christian the world over might be "off" in the same direction as Mr. Wang!

He was most public-spirited and zealous in the activities of his local church. The industrial school for country girls, opened in Man Ch'eng near his home, appealed to him as a worthy enterprise. As a practical expression of interest, he sold to the school quantities of vegetables from his garden at much below market price, and also offered his cart to take the teachers back and forth on errands to town and to haul coal and supplies for the school. He refused any compensation, but later as the pinch of a hard year began to be felt, the school staff insisted on paying the feed for his animals on the days used.

When difficulty was experienced in finding a satisfactory man to carry water and do marketing for the school, Mr. Wang offered to do it himself free of charge. It was ridiculous to pay such a price, he said. During the whole year he was the good angel of the school, daily working with a will to keep things running smoothly.

When I asked to take his picture, he modestly demurred.

"I am nobody but a simple, unlettered church member," he said. "What would anyone want of a picture of a rough old fellow like me?" Only the insistence of the school girls prevailed and he consented to be snapped.

Mrs. Yang

I never went to the Wan Hsien chapel but one of the first smiling faces to greet me was that of little old Mrs. Yang, seller of seeds. She fairly lived at the chapel and made herself useful in a thousand ways—running errands, keeping things clean, teaching beginners. If a strange Bible woman came to work for a time Mrs. Yang acted as a guide and escort to surrounding villages. Very humble service this, but it was done unto the Lord, and her reward may surprise some of us who feel more important!

CHAPTER 20

MRS. KAO

Mrs. Kao is a woman whose acquaintance was well worth cultivating. Physically of no mean proportions, she was almost as broad as she was tall, with a heart big enough to mother the whole world. Anyone in sorrow or distress had, by reason of that misfortune, a preferential mortgage on her interest and efforts. In this land of crushing poverty such labors were never lacking for her heart and hands.

For years she had been Bible woman extraordinary in the Paotingfu country field. Being herself a simple country woman, she thought nothing of the inconvenience of temporary lodgings, gladly enduring any hardship for the joy of bringing one more soul out of darkness into His marvelous light. And how she was beloved! She would need to multiply herself many times to accept half the pleading invitations that came to her.

Whenever Mrs. Kao's sympathetic heart was persuaded that someone ought to be helped, she developed in prayer a thorough and far-reaching plan. Then beginning her campaign, by persistent and persuasive means, she worked through to her desired end. If you were the one she was seeking to move and you happened to be opposed to her proposal, it was unfortunate, for you would eventually be doing as she desired. But usually it was a privilege to help in her sensible and beneficent schemes.

On one occasion she suddenly stated, "When Dr. Mackey returns and you start housekeeping again, you will need servants. Have they already been engaged?"

As Dr. Mackey's return was nearly a year distant, this did not seem pressing. But I assured her that, of course, Mrs. Liu and Yu Chin would come back to us when we needed them.

"But you haven't a sewing woman engaged, have you?" And then she unfolded her plan. In Man Ch'eng lived a widow with two small sons. Her husband had been an educated man and at his death schoolmates had raised a purse for this family, but the income from this source only helped a little toward the daily bread.

This widow had never had a chance to study much of the Truth, but seemed sincere in her interest. As she sat on her k'ang spinning or sewing to earn her living, she kept a hymn or text before her and pondered it as she worked. But the most remarkable thing about her—and here Mrs. Kao waxed even more enthusiastic—was her independence of spirit. No matter how straightened in circumstances, she never asked help of anyone but bravely met her problems herself. This was most unusual in China, where borrowing or begging from friends and relatives was nearly universal. And, in spite of her poverty, her little boys were kept neat and clean in their much-patched garments.

"Now," concluded Mrs. Kao briskly, "I think it would be fine if you would hire her as Dr. Mackey's sewing woman. She could learn more of the Lord in family prayers here, and not only would she be saved, but her two manly little sons could go to school here and become Christians too, and we would have saved the whole family!" How her face shone and her eyes sparkled as she outlined this much to be desired consummation.

Of course it was necessary to wait until Dr. Mackey's return and consult her wishes. But Mrs. Kao never allowed me to forget the little widow, and I'm sure she never allowed the Lord to forget either. So it came about that she had the pleasure of bringing the little family to Paotingfu, finding a place for them to stay, and getting them started in their new life. And we never regretted this addition to our household. I had no doubt the little mother would be ready for baptism as soon as she could read her Bible with greater ease. Wherever possible, we encouraged catechumens to be able to read before they entered the church, knowing that feeding on the Word was essential to growth in the Christian life.

The spring before, while on a tour of a mountain district, Mrs. Kao sent me word of encouraging growth among the Christians. Enclosed in her letter was a note of greeting written in phonetic by a little girl of twelve. This child's family was saved from starvation during the famine of 1920-21, and thereafter never seemed able to keep the wolf from the door. I had been struck with their bitter case on an earlier visit of my own to that section, but none of my suggestions for relief seemed practical. When this note arrived, one who was wise in the ways of Mrs. Kao said, "She has a plan for the Shih family. She is beginning her campaign." Personally, I was glad for they had been very much upon my heart and conscience.

When Mrs. Kao returned, she said, "We certainly must do something for the Shihs. They are absolutely without resource. Their clothes are old rags people have given them and they haven't enough to eat." (The Chinese expression used here is very forceful: "They cannot fill their food kettle.") But in spite of their desperate situation they maintained a humble faith of great beauty. When their heathen neighbors reproached them, saying, "You are Christians and yet are starving to death? We thought your God could take care of you," then Mrs. Shih replied, undaunted, "If it had not been that the Lord took mercy upon us, we would have been dead long ago."

I agreed relief should be given, but confessed I had found no suitable means. This was the opportunity Mrs. Kao wanted, and she proceeded to unfold her scheme. A leaders' class was about to convene in Paotingfu, and Mrs. Shih, the baby, and 12-year-old girl would come in at that time. In the meantime, Mrs. Kao would explain the situation to all her friends, Chinese and foreign, and take up their contributions whether large or small, thus accumulating a little capital with which Mrs. Shih could start in business.

I hesitated, suggesting that it hardly seemed wise to bring them to the city where there were already so many poor people and where living expenses were higher than the country. But the business which Mrs. Shih was to undertake was the making of a special kind of biscuits for which there would be no market in the country. Already a woman in the neighborhood who sold flour had agreed to undertake the sale of the new biscuits. And so it was arranged, and I hoped upon my return from vacation to learn that the market for Mrs. Shih's delectable product had been flourishing.

I am sure that this little glimpse of Mrs. Kao—a woman of faith and prayer and practical love—will stimulate many to pray for her that her boundless energy would always be directed in ways of His wisdom, and her love of souls would win hundreds to the Lord she loved and served.

CHAPTER 21

COVETING GIRLS

Loveable. That describes them—these women I met and came to know as I traveled for miles over the plains and up into the hill country, stopping for days or weeks in a score of villages and visiting in hundreds of homes.

There were the old ladies who had seen much of the tragedy of life. How wise they were, yet how ignorant! Well-read in the book of privation, learned in the blackness of the human heart, but completely unlearned of the things of the Spirit that made living beautiful and glorified the path of the humblest with eternal hope.

For example, Mrs. Wu. She was quiet and self-effacing, the castoff wife of a rich man. It is an old story: a beautiful and aggressive concubine, frightful quarreling, the older woman driven out without a penny. Efforts to interest her in the Good News only elicited the assertion, "My memory is too bad!"

An old blind woman came in. She was rather proud of the fact that she ruined her eyes in an outbreak of violent rage. Yes, the gospel is good, but she is too old; it is not for her. And no pleading seems to shake her from this fixed belief. Another was earlier quite interested, and then went back, overwhelmed by the misfortune of having no daughter-in-law to look after the house in her absence. And she couldn't trust the Lord to keep the thieves away while she went to church.

But there were more hopeful ones—those upon whom in the evening of their days has shined the light of the glorious gospel of Christ. How painstakingly they furrowed their brows over the simple gospel primers as they tried to memorize the blessed story. And they did so regret the long, weary, wasted years when they bowed down to sticks and stones. They were saved, but they had missed a lifetime of peace and joy and service.

So you see why my heart went out to these older ones. The tragic words "Too late!" seemed to be written on so many faces. Those whose hearts were opened to believe had to undo a whole lifetime of wrong thinking and wrongdoing.

As for the younger women, they came with babies in arms and tagging at their heels. Sweet children they were, but spoiled and untrained. These harassed mothers knew nothing of the working of a child's mind or of the principles of discipline. One fixed idea was that when a child cried he must be given something to eat, no matter what time it was or when he last ate. Or if a child displayed a bad temper, his mother brought forth a worse one with a torrent of angry abuse. They were loving and self-sacrificing, these mothers, but they simply lacked knowledge. Pathetic in their eagerness to hear and to learn, but almost handicapped by babies.

Then there were the young girls, bright faced and attractive, the hope of tomorrow. If only they could be saved from the hopelessness and misery of their grandmothers, if they could be prepared to become intelligent homekeepers and mothers. If only they could be started right and kept from having so much wrongness to un-live.

But how could they be pulled out of the rut worn for them by the feet of hundreds of generations? These were mission schools, where Opportunity beckons alluringly, but hundreds of these country girls couldn't afford even the modest fees required. In these families, from her birth a girl was considered a liability rather than an asset. Not because of a lack of love, but from economic necessity sons were desperately desired. A girl baby, no matter how sweet and loveable, was a burden on the family. She must be fed and clothed until of a marriageable age when she entered the home of her mother-in-law and the latter reaped the benefit of her strength and service.

One intriguing little miss of three was called "Little Brother." Another girl answered to "Exchange-for-a-brother," and yet another, "Call-a-son." Every mention of the names of these girls was a plea for the desired son, and the poor girls grew up in an atmosphere of being undesired, which lasted until they presented their husbands with sons.

American girls, with hundreds of interesting and useful vocations open to them, can scarcely appreciate the narrowness of outlook faced by thousands of their Chinese sisters. From the beginning unwanted, always looked down upon as a "know nothing," with none of the happy companionship of school days, no peep into the world of written words and books, none of the joy of preparing to be a worthwhile contributing member of society, no hope of understanding a little more fully and living a little more nobly than the failures of the past. And yet how much of future welfare lay in their hands! Do you wonder I coveted them for the Lord? Or that I coveted for them an opportunity to develop Christian character, intelligent minds, and skillful hands?

How could anyone live among them and hear their heart-moving appeals and not be stirred by action? For two years, some of us prayed, discussed, hoped, and planned. Plainly some sort of industrial school was needed where the girls could study half a day and work half a day to support themselves. This involved finding suitable buildings, capable teachers, a marketable handicraft, collecting materials, overseeing the work, and—most important—marketing the product. I was so convinced of the urgency of proclaiming the Good News that I begrudged any time spent on supplementary work, but when all the other difficulties appeared to be miraculously solved I could not refuse to take on this responsibility and try to give these girls a chance.

Buildings on a chapel property in the country at Man Ch'eng were easily adapted for the school. An elderly evangelist and his wife lived there and made ideal guardians for the girls. Two fine teachers appeared, one graduating from middle school and one from nurses' training school. The latter was able not only to look after the health of the girls, sanitation, nutrition, and so on, but she also was a very capable manager and dependable in the handling of funds.

The selection of the sort of work to be done was most difficult. Cross-stitch, applique, and embroidery work was being done so extensively that competition was keen. We finally decided to make Chinese cloth slippers for bedroom use. Practical and useful, they were something most Chinese girls knew how to make.

When notice of the opening of the school was sent around the country, we were flooded with applicants. Our present capacity was limited to 30, and no more could possibly be admitted until we ascertained whether it could be self-supporting. But it was a dreadful task to pick out the 30 who might attend, and still more painful to meet the scores of disappointed ones. We could only hold out the hope that if sales were good next year we would be able to enlarge. The happiness of the fortunate 30 could be seen from their picture which was taken, and one knows it is improper for a Chinese to smile when one's photograph is taken!

Some of the girls were too young to do very good work, but they learned. Two of them trudged 70 li to the school, and though they couldn't use a needle we hadn't the heart to send them home again. A number were motherless, thus having missed the training that Chinese women could impart. Others, because of distressing poverty, were farmed out as little slave girls. But all were tractable and loveable, and even these first three months of opportunity changed their outlook on life.

We trusted that the simple, practical teaching we offered would make them more useful to the Lord, to their homes, and to China, and that the school would be carried on if it was His will.

CHAPTER 22

PILLS AND POWDERS —
AND WHAT HAPPENED

Somewhere in the classic literature we all read in our youth, which we have now successfully forgotten, there was an expression to the effect that great things from small beginnings grow. This fact seems to be irrefutable when one considers the well-known relation between the tiny acorn and the mighty oak.

A new development now existed in the Paotingfu mission medical work which perhaps had not yet reached the oak stage, but was exhibiting such sturdy characteristics that one was filled with hope. It was no less than the Hsin An branch of the Taylor Memorial Hospital, an institution originated and supported wholly by local Chinese.

The acorn was planted as much as 20 years ago when the first itinerating country workers preached in this prosperous river town. The older inhabitants now laugh as they recall how curious they were about these foreign visitors and how afraid of them. No one dared to have anything to do with them, not even to rent them a room. But through prayer a foothold was at last secured and later a commodious property was bought for chapel and schools. From time to time a woman doctor accompanied the evangelist and held clinic in one of the chapel rooms. Equipment was simple— bottles and jars of pills and powders arranged on a rough table, and a row of enamel basins with antiseptic solutions on a wooden bench. Even with such facilities remarkable confidence was created in the doctor and her medicines.

Three years ago the foreign physician was unable to go, but she sent Dr. Tu, a capable Chinese girl with a beautiful

Christian character who had already been used of God in both her professional and spiritual ministry. It happened that the daughter of a very wealthy man became ill and sent for the doctor. The result was a grateful and appreciative patient. And it was this daughter who conceived the idea of providing a properly equipped hospital in Hsin An so the mission doctors might have a fit place to work while they were there.

Her father, being quite a philanthropist, at that time had set aside a certain sum of money to build a new bridge for the benefit of the community. Of this amount a substantial balance remained after the completion of the bridge, so the enterprising daughter urged that it be used for the hospital—which eventually happened. Two courts of finely built buildings situated on the main street near the chapel were purchased, and the doctors from Paotingfu were asked to recommend what each room should be used for and how it ought to be renovated and furnished.

When all was completed, a grand opening was arranged by the donor. Six foreigners and several Chinese from Paotingfu represented the mission. Special invitations had been sent to the head men for miles around, so with the Hsin An notables, a most representative crowd of educated and influential men gathered for the services which were held in the mission chapel with addresses of presentation and acceptance. Mr. Tung, the philanthropist, read his speech in dignified Wen Li, the literary language. It was wholly unintelligible to the common folk present, but all were properly impressed and could at least look intelligent and appreciative. The gentry were called upon for a few informal words and a humble representative likewise read a learned discourse. The response from the mission was made by Mr. Mather, the country evangelist. His colleagues were exceedingly proud of his scholarship and linguistic attainments which enabled him to speak fluently and forcefully in polished but understandable Chinese.

Following the service an inspection of the hospital was in order. The bright red front gate was draped with flags and hung with lanterns. Within was the gateman's room and a pleasant room for men patients. The inner court was protected from the street by an artistic wooden screen, a device common in Chinese arrangements. It was gained by entering a second gate and circling the decorative screen.

On the right was the dispensary, very professional and Western in its snowy white appointments, imposing medicine shelves, and well-equipped operating room beyond. Directly opposite was the women's waiting room, while a more imposing building at the end of the court afforded convenient accommodation for the visiting doctors and nurses.

This beautiful place, costing originally $4000 Mexican and $2000 more for repairs, was presented to Taylor Memorial Hospital in perpetuity, or so long as it was used for medical work. A younger brother of the donor gave on the spot a three-year contract promising to pay $50 a month toward the expenses of a monthly clinic of six days. But already these ambitious folk were looking forward to raising more money and having a resident physician.

After an inspection of the plant, the guests returned to the chapel where the hospital staff were hosts for a feast.

All this gave Christianity and the church a position of greater respect and influence in the community. The "Way" was everywhere highly spoken of. But alas, in their self-satisfaction there is no conviction of sin and hence no longing for a savior. "For you say, I am rich, I have prospered, and I need nothing; not knowing that you are wretched, pitiable, poor, blind, and naked" (Revelation 3:17 RSV). Only persistent prayer of the church of God on their behalf could enable us to buy up this opportunity for saving souls.

Faithful preaching was carried on through all the clinics so everyone who came for physical healing learned something of the cure for souls.

On the afternoon of the opening of the hospital the foreign guests were also invited to inspect the home of the Tungs. The grounds were laid out on an elaborate scale in accordance with the principles of Chinese landscape gardening. A lake of artistically irregular outline was the excuse for lovely winding bridges, rookeries, and teahouses built over the water. On an islet in the midst was a large hall where reposed in state the tablet of the revered father of the family. This dignified building held tables, chairs, and cabinets of rich woods deeply carved and inlaid with mother-of-pearl.

The present Mr. Tung was foreign in his tastes and built an imposing house in the foreign style, ostensibly to entertain his overseas guests. In spite of the upholstered living room furniture, foreign prints on the walls, and the gleam of brass beds in the bedrooms, he lived with his family in rooms of Chinese design. In an adjoining yard a light airy schoolhouse of several rooms was being completed as a free school for the town youth.

In spite of his fine qualities and good works, however, Mr. Tung himself was a most pitiable slave—bound by alcohol. It was said that after midday he was always in a drunken stupor. Though he knew he should stop drinking and had expressed such a desire, he was powerless in the grip of the evil one and had yet been unwilling to cry for help from above.

Mrs. Tung was a womanly woman who, I am convinced, was not far from the kingdom of heaven. It was on a subsequent visit that I really made her acquaintance. As the little Bible woman led me in to call one day, my heart failed me and I felt helpless before so august and unapproachable a person. I sent up a prayer that our visit would not be in vain. This was answered in a remarkable way as Mrs. Tung opened up her heart. Despite her wealth and position she was a woman of great sorrow. Her husband's drunkenness was one grief; his concubine was also a thorn in the flesh. The man realized he ought to send her away, but seemed not to have the moral courage to act. But most crushing of all was their son's worthlessness. This young man, the only hope of the family, led a dissolute life of drinking and gambling and even opium smoking. When this last vice was discovered by his father, he was summarily turned out and disinherited.

"Oh, if he would only change!" was the despairing cry of the mother.

I am sure the Spirit directed my thoughts that day to the Bible account of a rebellious prophet of olden days who was permitted to suffer much in order that the Lord might bring him to Himself and save him for a life of faith and service. As I read the story, Mrs. Tung moved to my side and followed the characters on the page, for she was an excellent reader. She was deeply interested, and as I applied the lesson to her own life, she exclaimed, "How clear it all is and how true! I believe that!"

Before we left I offered to pray for her loved ones, and her gratitude could scarcely find words for expression. I believe she was sincere in her hope that we might have further opportunity for unfolding the Word.

A little later we called on the sweet daughter-in-law who was driven out with her worthless husband. Hardly more than a child herself, she had endured much abuse and reviling during his drunken rages. Her cry, too, was, "Oh, if he would only reform, everything would be all right." We pointed her to the only Source of such power and hope and she seemed brightly interested.

Surely in all these contacts, in this freshly aroused interest, in these stirrings of conscience, the Lord was working for His own glory. Oh, for hearts to pray unitedly and perseveringly that this whole family may shake off the fetters that bind them and become free in Christ Jesus!

CHAPTER 23

VISIT TO JAPAN

The Japanese have an old proverb, "See Nikko and die." Now I have seen Nikko and when I die I'll know I've seen one of the loveliest spots on earth.

Besides having a feast of beauty, we got a tremendous "wallop" out of living in a Japanese inn, the Konishi Hotel, and actually eating and sleeping the way the Nipponese do.

We were seven—all "mishes" from Korea or China, except a Miss O'Shaunessy, secretary to the American minister in Peking. We arrived after dark, by taxi, for cars now supplanted the picturesque rickshaws all over Japan. Though cars were cheaper and faster, 15 miles an hour seemed to be about the speed limit for them. Few craved to be chauffeurs in Japan, for the traffic rules were strict and the pedestrian seemed always to have the right of way.

After being deposited at the door of the Konishi, we sat down on its broad doorstep to remove our shoes and put on leather toe-slippers which were supplied to us. Though the manager spoke some English, we were not shown our rooms until we had written a report for the police including our names, ages, nationalities, destination, and business. This information was required at frequent intervals all over Japan.

The hotel floors in the lobby and halls were of beautiful brown wood, polished to a mirror-like brilliance. No wonder shoes were not allowed!

Our rooms opened off a narrow porch bordering a beautiful garden where a small brook made fascinating music. At the door of our room we removed our slippers and stepped with stocking feet on the thick, soft matting. A doll-size chest of drawers and mirror comprised the furniture, except square pillows to sit on.

We ordered dinner, and tea was immediately served by a maid, colorful in bright kimono and black hair piled high. As we sat on our pillows in a hollow square about the room, individual tables of red lacquer about a foot high were brought in. Each table was set with two covered red lacquer bowls, one covered blue china bowl, a saucer of pickled vegetables, and a pair of new chopsticks.

The manner in which the tables were brought in seemed very important. The maid removed her slippers at the door, advanced a few steps, sank gracefully to her knees, placed the table on the floor before you, bowed gravely, then pushed it gently toward you.

The lacquer bowls contained piping hot soup with interesting bits of fish and vegetables. A few minutes later each of us received a side tray which held, to our amazement, a delicious steak and sliced tomatoes. (I am inclined to think this was a foreign dish especially prepared for us.) After everything had been cleared away, the maid sank to her knees in the center of the room and bowed with her face clear to the floor.

When the maid made up our beds, they consisted of three thick quilts piled one on top another on the floor. A white sheet followed and, for covering, a brightly-colored comforter with a freshly laundered white lining, made with sleeves! Evidently we were supposed to sleep with arms stretched out straight on either side. (We didn't.)

Walls, a fascinating part of a Japanese house, slid back and forth and were removable, making the rooms delightfully airy in summer. At night wooden doors were fitted into a groove at the outer edge of the porch. These, carefully locked, formed a protective outer wall of the house.

In the morning we looked out at the beautiful garden and the little brook tumbling down the hillside, emptying into a fountain bordered by two lifelike white heron. The arrangement of rocks, shrubbery, trees, and flowers was most artistic, while in the distance stood lovely green mountains.

Following breakfast we motored to Lake Chusenji, a lovely spot several thousand feet higher than Nikko. The last four miles of the way had 31 hairpin turns, besides numerous curves. Thickly forested mountains contained beautiful trees resembling oaks and maples, with views of gleaming waterfalls. The most famous is Kegon Fall, where a Japanese student—leaving a note to the effect that there was no solution to the riddle of life—committed suicide. His act apparently struck the imagination of Japanese young people and scores followed his example. Finally a simple Japanese Christian woman posted a sign by the waterfall, begging all considering suicide to first come to see her. Many found a purpose in life through her, and were saved for Christian service.

Along the lakeshore, many hotels were built by the Japanese, who love beauty and appreciate their scenic spots. Here we ate a picnic lunch, having found a bake shop which sold hot buns of various kinds. In addition, we found fruit—apples, peaches, and pears—in abundance, though more expensive than at home.

The next day we spent among the temples and shrines for which Nikko is famous. Tombs of two of Japan's famous men are here, together with many Buddhist and Shinto temples, all in a great park with wonderful avenues of giant cryptomeria trees. Words could not describe it. Suffice to say that the coloring— marvelous red lacquer, carvings, real gold foil used in their ornamentation—was simply dazzling.

On the return trip we hiked down the mountain in order to stop and enjoy the wonderful views, also avoiding the hairpin drive by car.

In our trip through Japan several things impressed me. One was the beauty of the carefully reforested mountains. Another, the lovely green rice fields which covered every bit of level ground. Then the prosperous look of the villages and farmhouses, the splendid efficiency of the railroad system with its courteous redcaps, the general kindliness and courtesy of the people, and the rapid Westernization of their style and dress. The wearing of foreign-style clothes was encouraged by the government, though most men wore their comfortable kimonos at home.

I came away with a friendlier feeling toward our Nipponese neighbors, and a real appreciation of their fine qualities.

But by far the best part was to get back to dear old China and the royal welcome of Chinese friends. This part of the country had been suffering from revolution, banditry, locusts, hailstorms, epidemics. We faced tremendous problems, but a nation was in the making, and it was glorious to have a tiny share in making that nation Christian.

PART 2

1931-1949

The years of Japanese aggression and
occupation. Collapse of the Republic, and a time of
Communist uprisings. Floods, fighting, and famine.

CHAPTER 24

AN ANSWER TO PRAYER

We were bursting with joy and praise and gratitude for a gracious answer to our prayers of many months! The day before, all of a sudden Dr. Mackey found that she could walk! It seemed as though someone had taken a knife and cut the cords that had bound her knees for nearly two years and now she could walk normally and could trip up and down stairs as she hadn't been able to do for two years.

The marvelous part of it was that it came just at the end of a two day journey on donkeys and mules, when I supposed she would be laid flat on her back from sheer weariness. Instead of that, when we got in Thursday afternoon about four o'clock, she cleaned up and went over to see the hospital folk. After supper, she went to prayer meeting and stayed to a social afterward. For much of the time the past two years she had been unable to go to prayer meeting and still less to social functions. I scarcely felt able after our trip to go myself, so I was thoroughly surprised that she went at the close of such a hard day.

Then, instead of being tired out the next day, to have her knees all well! We were certainly full of praise.

The night before we left Kuan Tso Ling, I awoke at 12:10 a.m. and kept waiting for the mules to arrive. When they finally did, it was only 2:20. I hopped out and dressed hurriedly, but the men didn't come up to pack for a couple of hours, so I had to get into bed again to keep warm. Though the animals started off before six a.m., the work of closing up the house for the summer kept Dr. Mackey for another half hour.

Then we walked down the mountain. Dr. Mackey walked fully four miles, down a steep rocky road, with one hand holding a stick and the other on my shoulder. It appeared to be hard for her and I was almost wishing we had had her carried down in a chair. But later she said she believed that all the strain and the jar of the trip loosened up the adhesions in her knees and set them free.

One thing that made me so elated was that when she would go on furlough the next spring, all nice and well, there would be no question about her coming back. Our hearts had been heavy for fear that if she went home so crippled and the condition were permanent, they would probably not allow her to return. So we were thankful for more than just her release from pain and suffering. How gracious is our God!

Christian leaders and missionaries
(Florence front row third from left)

CHAPTER 25

LAUNCHING OUT IN PAOTINGFU
(1-8-32)

"Launch out into the deep,
and let down your nets for a draught"
(Luke 5:4).

That was the word with which our Lord sent us forth in October, and we were gratefully amazed at the draught of fishes He gave us.

Our first "fishing ground" was the Wan Hsien chapel where more than 40 women studied for two weeks. Most were Christians, some of many years' experience. The teaching was along the line of freedom from sin and hearts made clean and holy in His sight. Thirsty ones were led to experience the cleansing floods of the blessed Spirit's power.

First, Mrs. Tu confessed with tears of repentance the sin of not loving her daughter-in-law. She had always disliked her and quarreled with her constantly. I am sure there was joy in the presence of the angels when these two women knelt together, confessed to the Lord, and asked for a new heart of mutual love. They then begged each other's forgiveness, and soon they had the Spirit's witness in their hearts that a real transaction had taken place.

Would it last in the rub of daily life at home? We committed them trustfully to the Lord and two months later we heard their joyous testimony. All things had been made new. Only once had the mother-in-law been provoked into reviling the younger woman, but immediately she was convicted of sin, and that evening at family prayers she asked the Lord's forgiveness and that of her daughter-in-law. We praised His name together.

Mrs. Chou had made much trouble in the church through a fancied grievance against one of the Bible women. For months she carried a knife with the avowed purpose of venting her hatred on Mrs. Kao. Much prayer had been offered for this poor woman so obviously ensnared by the evil one. After several persons earnestly dealt with her, during the class every barrier was broken down. She recognized and confessed her sin to the Lord, publicly asking the church to forgive her. When she sought for a clean heart, her changed face gave evidence of a new work of grace as she testified to the peace of God which filled her being.

Mrs. T'sai had been a church member for years, yet probably not born again. While away working for her living, she had let months and years slip by without ever praying. But at last she came into vital contact with her Lord and all things became new.

Though the class was dismissed the day before we left, a number insisted on waiting to see us off before returning to their homes. One such was Mrs. T'eng. Her face shone as she told us, "I didn't come to this class in vain. I really repented and was saved a good many years ago. But now I know I must use love to win my daughter-in-law and family. Hereafter I'll stay home on Sunday and let them go to church." This decision was a real sacrifice, but attended by her prayers, I was sure it would bear fruit.

The prayer meetings were blessed times when we met together with the Lord. A new book of Scripture choruses printed in the phonetic proved a great treasure, as we literally sang the Word into the hearts and memories of many who had found reading laborious. Soon we acquired a second book of longer songs, printed with parallel columns of Chinese character and phonetic. Those who had mastered the first book could read this one without great difficulty, and with patience learned to recognize a large number of characters as well. Our experience the past months had shown that these little books were quite an advanced step to help our women and girls toward literacy.

After this, four small donkeys carried us and our baggage to K'ang Kuan. This is not strictly accurate, for I preferred to walk almost all the way. Though K'ang Kuan was a new place where no women evangelists had ever worked, we were graciously received in a wealthy home. This family proved to be relatives of a girl who had studied nursing in Paotingfu, so we had a good point of contact. But though many girls and young women came to see us, they were supercilious and it took many days before they became interested in learning to read and sing, and later to love to listen to the gospel. As they finally made big strides, some passed from death into life. The father of one of the girls who showed great interest—even writing a letter later full of praise for the wonderful salvation found in Jesus Christ—wants his daughter to enter Bible school next term. Thus we hoped for permanent results from our visit.

A number of poor distressed ones sought Miss Chao for medical aid, and several of them destroyed their idols and trusted in the true God.

Next we had promised to visit Shui Yo, the home of Mrs. Chang who had walked 30 miles to Paotingfu to attend our fall rally. But days passed and the Shui Yo people did not come to K'ang Kuan to make arrangements for our visit. We sent them a letter by a stranger going in that direction, but could not be sure it would reach them. The day for leaving came but we still had no word. After much prayer, Miss Chao and I decided to go ourselves to Shui Yo, and if all were well, to send back for Mrs. Li and the baggage.

We did not know the way and the mountain paths were hard to follow. Just as we started, however, a new acquaintance came along who was going close to our destination, so we had a guide.

About halfway we met Mr. Chang, coming with pack animals to get us. By a miracle he had received our letter, even though the name, address, and purport of the message had all been changed en route. Fortunately, just in time, he met one of the men evangelists who told him our plans, and he started out to fetch us on the proper day without regard to the misleading letter.

Shui Yo was the narrowest valley I had ever seen. The highway—a stony creek bed—ran down the middle, with room on either side for just one courtyard, a great rocky cliff forming the back wall. The sun became visible at eleven o'clock in the morning and disappeared behind a Western peak at three o'clock.

The villagers had a unique means of communication. They never troubled to hunt up the person they wished to talk to; they merely let out a shout. The mountains acted as a loudspeaker. The person addressed would respond and they would transact their business.

While there we lived in a house built by prayer. During the famine year the Changs had fled into the mountains and eked out an existence for some years. There they heard the gospel and Mr. Chang believed. Returning home they found their house tumbled down, but their family, who opposed their faith, refused to help them. After committing his troubles to God, Mr. Chang was moving an old broken cupboard when two silver dollars rattled down. He accepted them as the Lord's answer and used them as capital to start a little business selling buns. Normally there would have been little sale for them in that tiny valley. But just then a war scare sent in a host of refugees, and in about 20 days he cleared more than $30, a truly large sum, which enabled him to build a good house.

Mr. Chang hung out a gospel flag while we were there. Across the street an old woman had a rival banner—a little red flag. It indicated she was in communication with demons and could exorcise diseases for a certain remuneration. We prayed much for her, and she actually came to listen and was willing to learn a prayer. We hoped she would be delivered from the power of the evil one.

Our two weeks in Hsi Pai Shan seemed like days of heaven on earth. They had heard the gospel just a year before, and a large earnest group studied faithfully. Many clearly settled their sin account and witnessed to the joy of a clean heart. They were eager to know how to pray so they might have the assurance that God heard. Each carried burdens for relatives and friends they longed to see saved. In answer to the prayers of their mothers, several young men became keenly interested in the gospel.

It was blessed to see the working of the Spirit in hearts as one after another would inquire how to make things right that had been wrong in their past lives. Full of gratitude and joy, they would exclaim, "We didn't understand before; now we know!"

Our next visit was really two in one. We lived in "South End," but Miss Chao and I took turns going daily to "Big Village" a mile away to teach a group there. Though our hostess knew Christ, her family had never heard much of the gospel. Her father-in-law was a "master of wind and water," learned in geomancy, and much consulted as to lucky locations for graves, gates, and so on. He was most courteous to us, though I am sure the gospel did not mix well with his business. But several other members of his family seemed to accept the truth, and a granddaughter came back to Paotingfu with us to study for a month.

In Big Village we taught daily in the home of Mrs. Li. She had heard the gospel only six months before but had been convinced immediately of its truth. Formerly a worshiper of many idols, to acquire merit she had prepared countless offerings of food, and had knelt motionless while long sticks of incense slowly burned out. With tears in her eyes, she exclaimed, "I worshiped them as though they were true. But oh, I was never satisfied, never at peace. I kept longing for something better." This dear woman's heart had been prepared beforehand by the Lord for the coming of the gospel.

Though she was most anxious for her granddaughter to come in for a month's class, the parents were unwilling. Before we left, Mrs. Li said, "You are managing this class in Paotingfu, aren't you?" I replied that each of us had some responsibility for it.

"Well, I want to help," she told me, thrusting a dollar into my hand. This was a large gift for one in her circumstances. So many of us, I thought, have known the gospel all our lives and been more or less indifferent to it, but this woman had been waiting, hungering, and thirsting after the true God.

"Dear Lord," I prayed that evening, "quicken our lagging steps that we may speedily reach those dear ones you have already marked for your own, that the number of your elect may soon be completed, and you may indeed come quickly." Indeed, I wished we all might offer our adoration and praise for His wonderful salvation, who is "able to save to the uttermost."

CHAPTER 26

REVIVAL IN PAOTINGFU (1-29-32)

Revival had come! The Lord gloriously entered into His purified temple, and streams of living water freely flowed, bringing floods of joy into parched and thirsty lives.

For so many years we had prayed, "Lord, revive your church, and first, revive me." Now we could only praise Him who had done abundantly above all we had asked or thought.

It had been popular recently to urge missionaries to be learners, with minds open to receive all the fine things in other religions, willing to be taught by the people whom they visited. But I praise the Lord that He gave us a much more blessed experience than that. I was led into the deep things of the Spirit of God by one of this land to whom I had come as an ambassador of Christ. Pastor Chi had verily been both our Aquila and Priscilla, expounding unto us more perfectly the way of God. It was wonderful!

We had heard only vaguely of the Bethel Band of evangelistic workers before the Lord led them to us on January 13 for 12 days of meetings. Pastor and Mrs. Chi and Miss E, the song leader who accompanied them, all seemed so very young when we first met them. But we were soon reminded, "Let none despise thy youth," for the Lord Himself was with them in power.

Miss E was a gifted song leader, and the choruses still ring in my ears as a very precious heritage from the meetings: "Come and Dine," "Glorious Freedom," "Fill Me Now," "Jesus Breaks Every Fetter," and many others. Also every afternoon she led a meeting for outsiders, where there were daily decisions for Christ.

The preaching was not unusual, but the fruitage was. One woman who had been prayed for and worked with for 18 years, but had hardened her heart and persecuted her believing nieces, was won by the theme "As you please." Nine were saved in that one family during the meetings and their home transformed, the work of 18 years suddenly coming to fruition. Why? Simply because the Holy Spirit was able to work through cleansed instruments.

The early believers "lifted up their voice to God with one accord," and this method of the whole assembly praying aloud together proved wonderfully helpful to new believers, to the timid, and to those unused to praying in public. The sound of many voices importunately pleading for blessing encouraged others to seek also. It was a new experience to cold and dignified Presbyterians, but we grew to love it.

It had been my privilege to hear many fine preachers, having sat most profitably under those whose names were best known in England and America. Yet never had I been more refreshed than by the ministry of Pastor Chi. He had not been trained in college or seminary or Bible school, but instead, like Paul, he was deeply taught in God's own school. He was strictly a Bible preacher, expounding a whole chapter, paragraph by paragraph, in nearly every sermon. He preached with a blackboard, on which he drew comical but effective illustrations. By means of these pictures, plus his voice and action, he made the situation forcefully live before his audience.

One night Pastor Chi made the road to the cross and the scene on Golgotha stand out in a marvelous way. The next evening his theme was the raising of Lazarus and he had the audience convulsed with laughter many times. At first I feared he was too facetious to get results. But to my amazement, at the close of the service almost the whole congregation—nurses, Bible women, students, church leaders—went forward to seek the new birth!

One of the graduate nurses brought up in our schools and church, for years a Christian leader, declared that for the first time she understood what it meant to be born again. Yet regeneration had been taught and preached over and over. How to explain it? Simply! At last the Holy Spirit had taken the things of Jesus and showed them to us. How the angels in heaven must have rejoiced at all that was happening.

Pastor Chi looked like a mere youngster though he was actually 30 years old. But he was a marvelous preacher and through the Spirit opened the Word in a wonderful way. As he preached, one was impressed that he is passionately in love with the Lord and makes the cross stand out in a powerful picture. Of all the splendid preachers I had heard in English and Chinese, I had never heard any to surpass him.

Listening to this dear young man was a continual refreshment as, with a surprising insight into the Word, he brought out of every passage some altogether fresh interpretations.

In addition, Pastor Chi was a veritable clown! Can you imagine such a combination? He acted just like a kid, chasing around, acting out his presentations, but he soon turned the smiles into serious channels. He had an effective pleading voice.

Strange to say, he couldn't sing, though he had a tremendous booming speaking voice. Since he couldn't carry a tune, his wife and Miss E quickly piped up to carry on the choruses he started.

One afternoon when the team designated two to four o'clock to see individuals with spiritual problems, scores turned up. It was the greatest revival I had ever seen. The preaching was so clear step by step. All of us were definitely blessed.

At the last meeting when everyone who had made a decision was asked to come up front, 72 did so. The spiritual victories of older believers were remarkable and blessed. There was much cleaning house, with many apologies made and wrongs made right. Our own Pastor Ku immediately made plans to have Pastor Chi return the next fall for a retreat to which representatives would be invited from all over the province. Dr. Ku's faith was wonderfully strengthened, and at the end of the revival, he seemed 10 years younger.

CHAPTER 27

THE WAY OF PASTOR CHI

Pastor Chi Chih Wen came from a very poor home. His father died when he was little and his mother supported the children—himself and two small sisters—by spinning and weaving. He knew what it was to go hungry to school.

In 1923 he saw the Bible for the first time. In 1925 he was called to preach. By that time he had a good position in the postal service. His mother reproached him for giving up this lucrative work, forgetting her years of weary toil for the family. It was a great sorrow to him. But he dreamed he saw himself in a coffin, dead, and when he awoke, he determined to die to self. A friend helped him finish his high school course.

Once he went through the rain a long distance to keep a preaching appointment. He was drenched to the skin, and going home, he had to wade through water knee-deep with the stones cutting his feet. The devil questioned, "Is it worthwhile?" but the Lord graciously blessed him and his heart was filled with peace and with the Holy Spirit.

Later while away on a preaching tour one of his sisters was taken ill. Because they did not realize she should be sent to the hospital, she was beyond hope when he returned home. That was a great sorrow, but he joyfully shouldered the cross, and his heart was filled with the Holy Spirit.

The basis for Pastor Chi's morning sermons during our revival in Paotingfu was the Gospel of Luke, as this professedly is written as a guide to heaven. Each chapter marks a distinct step on the journey: repentance, regeneration, baptism of the Holy Spirit, sanctification, being full of the Spirit, how to walk the way of holiness. Each evening he expounded on the same theme from a different portion of Scripture. This teaching method was wonderfully thorough and helpful. Since the Holy Spirit used these messages to bring wonderful blessing to scores, they are briefly outlined here:

Luke 1

Written to a man of importance (vv. 1-4). Every unsaved person feels self very important. The theme of the chapter is repentance, for John was the representative of repentance.

Zacharias was versed in the law (vv. 5-7) and knew that the "wages of sin is death."

He was given a vision of God's holiness which inevitably makes one realize his own sin (vv. 8-23). Yet instead of crying with Isaiah "Woe is me," he doesn't repent. He knows he ought to repent, but when he doesn't believe, he becomes dumb. So with many Christians. They know they ought to repent but are unwilling, so their lips are closed and they have no testimony.

As the coming of the longed-for son "put away" Elizabeth's reproach (vv. 24-25), so repentance puts away the sinner's shame.

The grace of God helps us to come to repentance (vv. 26-35). Forgiveness awaits the repentant.

Mary takes up the cross of the world's disdain, her three months with Elizabeth indicating her own repentance (vv. 36-55).

As soon as his father names the babe John, recognizing him as the representative of repentance, his mouth is opened and he praises God (v. 56). So every repentant one has a testimony of praise.

Luke 23:26-43
The Salvation of the Cross
The groups from around the cross:

Simon from the country unwillingly bore the cross (v. 26). Because he didn't know its meaning, he was unsaved.

An unsaved multitude follow (v. 27). The women weep, but not for their own sins.

Two thieves on the cross with the Lord, yet without any spiritual relationship to the cross; not trusting in the cross (v. 32). Typical of those who sacrifice themselves for humanity, yet without faith in cross they are unsaved.

The soldiers saw the Lord nailed to the cross, yet were unsaved (v. 34). They were busy dividing his garments. They believed in money.

The rulers wanted to see a miracle before they would believe (v. 35). The scoffers wanted a cross-less salvation.

In all this multitude only one was saved. If such a criminal can be saved, why haven't we been saved?

The thief heard the trial and wondered that the Lord was speechless in his own defense; and still more that Pilate himself pronounced Him without fault. He saw the Lord willing to bear the cross until exhausted. He questioned why the women cry for the Lord. "No one cries for me; even my own mother reviles me." He saw the Lord willing to be nailed to the cross while the thieves fought and cursed and struggled. He was amazed at the gracious prayer that came from the Lord's lips in place of reviling.

How was the thief saved?
1. He recognized his own sin.
2. He reproved himself for his own sin. He was unwilling to confess before the judge even though beaten repeatedly. He kept averring his own innocence until on the cross he saw the Lord, and confessed.
3. He confessed his own sin and his faith in the Lord; no one in all that multitude had a good word to say for Jesus but this thief.
4. He left his sin.
5. He prayed—only three phrases but they opened the gate of heaven, shut the gate of hell, and moved the Lord's heart. Why so powerful? Because they came from the heart.

6. He believed the Lord's word—"Today shalt thou be with me in paradise"—for the thief had nothing more to say or desire.

Luke 2
The Second Step on the Road to Heaven

Being born again is having the Lord's life born within us. If He is not living in us, we are unsaved.

The crowd of people who returned to Bethlehem for the registration were full of worldly affairs, some eager for revolution, some bent on business advantage. Only these two, Mary and Joseph, were full of what God was fulfilling in them. They were eager to see this child, their hearts empty of all else.

1. If we want the Lord in our hearts, we must first empty them. The Lord is seeking an empty place. It may be only a humble heart into which He will come even as into the stable, while He passes by the heart that is full of the world, even as the inn. "Blessed are the pure in heart" (Matthew 5:8).

2. The shepherds in the cold, dark desert places were sleepless because of concern for their flocks. Typical of those in this world of sin who are concerned for others. The angels brought to them comfort: "The Lord has come; the Lord has a way to save." Is your heart comfortless? It is because you have never wept for sinners. "Blessed are they that mourn; for they shall be comforted" (Matthew 5:4).

3. Those shepherds were childlike in their simplicity and faith. They never doubted but said, "We'll go and see." With childlike unconcern they left their sheep to go. Born-again persons think of His things first. "Blessed are the meek; for they shall inherit the earth" (Matthew 5:5). "Seek ye first the kingdom of God, and his righteousness, and all these things shall be added unto you" (Matthew 6:33).

4. Mary and Joseph wanted to fully follow God's will. They didn't choose a name for the Baby themselves. "Blessed are they who do hunger and thirst after righteousness; for they shall be filled" (Matthew 5:6).

5. They presented Him to God. Those not born again only pray for themselves, their family, their business, and for peace. They give the useless to the Lord. The born-again one gives his best to God. Put your precious things in heaven. If you love money, give it to the Lord.

6. Only Simon and Anna recognized the Lord, because they were pure in heart. The born-again one rejoices to see the Lord.

Evening Message
Regeneration

Bethany is the place of communion with the Lord. But Lazarus was sick with "chills and fever" because the Lord was not in his heart. Chills and fever indicate the fluctuations of the Christian experience of many.... Trouble drives to prayer, to send and tell the Lord. We can pray boldly, for it is for the one that He loves.

The disciples feared to go with the Lord; they were afraid of the cross; afraid the stones would also be hurled at them. The Lord admonished them that with the Light of the World, they need not fear.

Lazarus was in the grave and couldn't return home—typical of sinners in the world who can't return to the heavenly home. A cave is an empty place. Men don't realize this world is empty because they are blinded by money.

If Lazarus' family wanted him raised, they must roll away the stone—of sin—and believe. His own sister said, "He decayeth." Your family knows your condition. Marks of the unsaved: They are in the world, their sin is not confessed, they are dead. The born-again one comes out from the grave of the world, leads others, and bears the cross (John 12:10). The rulers seek to put Lazarus to death.

Luke 3
The Baptism of the Holy Spirit
  Preparation for the Baptism (vv. 1-6)
1. Fill up the valleys of unbelief; the promise is for you (Galatians 3:14).
2. Level the mountains of pride and self-righteousness and self-dependence.
3. Make straight the crooked motives, not really willing to bear the cross.
4. Make the rough places smooth, the alternating hot and cold spiritual temperature becomes even.

  Necessary Qualifications (vv. 7-14)
Must be a stone made into a son, one who has passed from death to life may receive. Born-again ones cease from sin and share with others.

  Nature of the Baptism of the Holy Spirit (vv. 15-17)
To be born again is to be baptized with water, to have sins forgiven.

To be baptized with the Holy Spirit is to be baptized with fire, burning clean our motives, by strong disinfectant destroying the sin germ. The chaff is burned with fire.

  Results of the Baptism of the Holy Spirit:
Not afraid of the cross; willing to reprove all of sin (vv. 18-20).

One is as concerned for the sins of others as though they were one's own (vv. 21-22).

If baptized with the Holy Spirit, have an inheritance with the sanctified (vv. 23-28).

Evening Message
Hindrances to the Baptism of the Spirit

John 4

The disciples rush off to eat while the Lord waits to save. Unwilling to give so much as a drink to the Creator of all. Today He thirsts for loving hearts.

The gift of God is the Lord Jesus and the Holy Spirit (v. 10).

The woman knew too well the weary round of eternally being unsatisfied (v. 15)

The Lord knew the woman's secret sin (v. 18). Why had these five husbands died one after another? They were done to death because all the time she had another man: sin. The same people return to the Lord in consecutive revival meetings, only to grow cold again. Why? Because of sin. This "husband" must be turned over to the Lord before He can give the living Water.

Don't depend on feelings. If you have given all sin to the Lord, just believe He has given the Holy Spirit.

I believe God has given me His Holy Spirit (John 1:16) and I want to witness daily.

Sanctification
1 Thessalonians 5:23-28

The Bible teaching on holiness is very complete. It is mentioned 900 times, which is many more times than repentance or regeneration.

1 Thessalonians 4:3

We pray "Thy will be done." That will is for us to be sanctified.

1 Peter 1:15

"Be ye holy." This is His command. We can't keep all his commands and fail in one. The Lord has two calls: He calls sinners to repent; He calls believers to be sanctified.

1 Thessalonians 5:23

"The God of peace sanctify you wholly." This is for those who have already received peace. Born-again ones long for holiness. To be born again is the first step on the road of holiness. It is God's work. How?

By blood (Hebrews 13:12)

By the Holy Spirit (Romans 15:16)

By the Word (John 17:17)

It is all prepared; if we fail to receive, it is our own fault. To be sanctified does not mean that one cannot sin but that one is enabled *not* to sin.

A gun in the hands of a bandit is used to destroy; in the hands of a policeman it is used to protect. We in the hands of Satan are used to sin; in the hands of God to be holy.

How do we receive it?

Ask (Luke 11:13)

Believe (Acts 26:18)

Evening Message
Sanctification
Hebrews 12:14-16

Unless you are born again, you can't see the kingdom; unless you are sanctified, you can't see the Lord. Only Anna and Simon saw the Lord in the temple, because they were sanctified. The unholy cannot enter the New Jerusalem.

Sanctification is hindered by the root of bitterness transmitted from Eve (v. 15). It is the seed of the viper in our hearts (self: Matthew 16:24). It is this self that sins. In the sanctified one's self is on the cross.

The second hindrance is love of the world (v. 16). The world must be put on the cross. We can't have both. If we cling to the world, we will lose son's heritage. The Lord must take the place in our hearts of self and the world.

How Do We Become Sanctified?
1. Put down every burden, every worry (Philippians 4:6)
2. Lay aside besetting sins.
3. Entire consecration.
4. Look to Jesus.

If our eyes are on Him, we can't see money or material advantage; if our eyes are on Him, we do not fear for we can't see other people's slights and offenses.

> "Looking to Lord Jesus
> Daily looking to the Lord
> The world and self nailed to death,
> Sanctified, going the heavenly way
> Looking to the Lord Jesus."
> (Rough translation of a helpful chorus sung to the tune "Down at the Cross.")

Luke 4

Full of the Spirit

When Jesus came up from the Jordan, i.e., death, He came in the power of a resurrected life. Only one who has received newness of life and who has been sanctified can be full of the Holy Spirit. A sanctified one still has temptations but now has the power to overcome them.

There is no need to seek for a sign of sanctification. It comes by faith (vv. 9-12).

The work of an evangelist consists of:

1. Casting out devils—liberating from sin.

2. Healing the sick—leading believers to become sanctified.

The devil-possessed one was in the temple, i.e., unsaved ones within the church.

How to Be Full of the Spirit

One hundred twenty disciples waited for the Spirit's power; 380 went without waiting, but we don't hear of their winning converts.

They waited in the upper room, separated from the world; in the room where they ate the last supper, a room sacred with thoughts of the Lord, where before their eyes was the seat where He sat, the cup He blessed, etc.

There they were also reminded of Judas, the "Big I". The Big I is the greatest hindrance to being filled with the Spirit. It took 10 days to put "I" on the cross before the Holy Spirit could come. Then they were enwrapped in the Holy Spirit. In that room the Lord had divided His body and blood for His disciples; now He divides His Spirit. He came as a new tongue, not their own but holy from heaven.

1. More dead to self, more full of the Holy Spirit. Being full of the Spirit must result in people either repenting or hating you.

2. More witness-bearing, more full of the Spirit.

3. More prayer, more full of the Spirit.

> The more we pray, the more humble we become (Acts 4:23-24).
>
> The more we pray, the more we understand the Bible (vv. 25-27).
>
> The more we pray, the more we care for the sins of others (v. 28).
>
> The more we pray, the more we know God's will.

4. More cross-bearing, more full of the Holy Spirit.

Stephen preached from Genesis to Revelation in his longing for their conversion (Acts 7:54-56). The Lord Himself arose to welcome His faithful servant.

Luke 5
How to Win Men

The empty boat is typical of the heart empty and willing to be used by the Lord. Jesus was in the midst and yet not stained with the world. Peter was willing to be taught. We must have a deep experience ourselves before we can help others.

1. We must call others to share the blessing we have ourselves received (v. 6). The boat didn't sink, for His grace is sufficient.

2. Peter emptied his heart by confession (v. 8); then the Lord said, "Thou shall catch men."

Qualifications of an evangelist—empty of self and full of God. Launch out into the deep:

The city (v. 12), spiritual lepers

The home (v. 17), paralyzed ones

On the road (v. 27)

Heart must be full of love to draw (v. 13)

Must be faithful (v. 21); don't fear opposition or
  persecution.

Must be warm-hearted, fired by the Holy Spirit.

The Lord is with all who obey and teach as He
  commanded (v. 34).

Acts 3:1-10
How To Walk the Holy Way.

The lame one can't help others; he himself must be borne. He is daily carried but only to the outside of the door. We bring many to join the church but not into the company of born-again ones. We are very busy, but we get nothing fundamental done. These bearers of the lame ones have great faults:

1. Lack of harmony

2. Discouragement—this is Satan's best weapon

3. Unwilling to bear the cross to the end.

4. Self lame in one foot, either not born again or not sanctified.

Lame ones can't escape
Lame ones can't kneel to pray

Who is this beggar? The one who knows only to take and not give. He only prays for self; doesn't give witness for the Lord.

Lame ones can't do the will of the Father (Matthew 7:21). If they hear and don't do, they become so fat from over-eating they can't be moved.

Cure for lameness:

1. Look to the Lord. "Look on us."
2. Be separated from the world. He jumped up.
3. Give self to the Lord. Go forward. Forget home, loved ones, in zeal for God.

Luke 18

Pray Without Ceasing

We can change situations by prayer when everything else fails. Why should this widow be so importunate? Because she had no husband to depend on. Who is "husband"? Self. If you are still depending on self, you will not pray without ceasing.

At the opening of each sermon Pastor Chi explained briefly his theme, and then asked the audience to pray aloud together, each person for himself that he might receive this blessing. Then at the close there would be united prayer again and raising of hands by those who believed God had heard their prayers and gave the blessing they were seeking. In this way every message was made immensely practical and personal and no one could dodge the issue. We were led definitely and joyfully each step of the way.

In the last few meetings a brief period was given for testimonies. Only very short ones were encouraged, but such a lot of joy packed into a few words: many who had definitely settled their sin account and who knew they were born again; some rejoiced in cleansed hearts; others gladly took up the cross as their glory. Many were conscious that fetters had been broken, that the Lord was reigning where self and the world had had dominion. So many sad, burdened faces were transformed with an inner shining that was glorious to see.

At the close of one meeting as Pastor Ku announced an early morning prayer meeting, he remarked, "Pastor Chi says my faith is small. I know it is. But I want to be a man of great faith." Few noticed that after those words, Pastor Ku knelt in a dark corner at the rear of the church weeping brokenly. But the next day his shining face indicated that the Lord had given him a new name—not Jacob but Israel! In numerous ways the transformation revealed itself. "I have been depending on myself; now I am entirely in the Lord's hands," was his testimony.

To conserve the results of the meetings, Pastor Chi organized a Prayer Tower. The plan was to have at least one person every hour there to pray for all the prayer requests that were sent in. Also a large number of small evangelistic bands were organized, each to go out once a week. And a new impetus was given to family worship.

We knew that the same Holy Spirit who had begun this good work would carry it on. And we separated, "looking to Jesus" for continual victory.

CHAPTER 28

PRAYER WORKS MIRACLES (MAY 1932)

I knew friends had been praying, for the Lord had been working miracles, the kind that "goeth not out but by prayer."

Our little Bible Institute had a glorious year, blessed above all we asked or thought. The year before, after the Lord gave us 40 students, the spiritual thermometer of the school kept rising. Since having a quiet time with the Lord became impossible in the crowded dormitories, the students themselves prepared a prayer room that blessed everyone all through the term. Many temptations were overcome and burdens left there.

The furnishings, all the students' idea, had yellow curtains at the windows, while about the room stood benches with yellow cushions to kneel upon. A simple table in front, also draped in yellow, bore a wooden cross. Several prayer promises decorated the walls. Simple, yes, but it had a holy, worshipful atmosphere.

In the preceding fall the Lord sent over 60 students, and in November a revival began among them, starting with a girl grammar school graduate from Peking. Unhappy at first, she cried and complained she didn't understand why God had brought her here. She wanted to go to high school and not waste her time among these illiterates.

A classmate finally led her to Miss K'ung for prayer and counsel, where the Lord graciously dealt with her. With tears she confessed her sins were many. At 12 years of age she had repented but then grew cold, loving the world and fancy clothes, and even stealing to gratify her desires. Then she began to make restitution and ask forgiveness.

The students felt moved that she was willing to "lose face" by public confession, and then by her wonderful joy. Little

groups of two and three began to seek out their teachers saying, "We want to be born again." Their confessions were very
real as, convicted by the Holy Spirit, they renounced their sins
with tears.

As these found peace, others followed. Sin was dealt with
and joy resulted. There was much asking of pardon from fellow students, teachers, pastor, and missionary friends. They
confessed falsehoods, stealing, reviling, criticism, even unkind
words. One girl made a special trip home to ask forgiveness of
her mother. Her humble confession so moved the family, they
soon all sought salvation, confessing their sins with tears. Even
the day school received similar blessings.

In the Bible school only a little group of five remained
who hardened their hearts. One declared she would rather go
to hell than confess her sins. Two day school teachers also remained untouched, but in January even these were saved.

Following this outpouring, every Sunday afternoon five
evangelistic bands began to go out preaching in homes, street
chapels, or surrounding villages. They grew by sharing. The
influence of one life wholly yielded to God cannot be com-
puted. As we gave Him adoration and praise for blessings past,
we looked trustfully to Him for greater victories in the future.

CHAPTER 29

BANDITS AND MUDDY STREAMS (8-1-32)

We planned to hike up Cow Temple Mountain one morning, but we were awakened by terrific thunder instead. Though we thought it would continue for weeks, it cleared in a surprisingly short time. However, we still didn't get our hike.

Friends came from town about the middle of the morning with news that the city of Hai Shen Shan was in an uproar. Roving bandits were about 70 li south. Even the county official and his family had fled, along with the head of the bureau of public safety. People were on the run, but didn't know where to go.

Marvelous are the mercies of the Lord. After a trip of special providences, we arrived safe and sound in Liu Chia Chuang and had our usual meetings, given over largely to testimonies. The Lord worked in many hearts and some cold and backslidden ones made humble confession of sin and testified to forgiveness.

In the morning news came that the bandits, mostly communists, were only eight li away. A band of cavalry sent to quell them joined them instead, so their numbers were formidable.

When news came that the worst was over and we could go, the whole crowd rolled their trousers to their hips to help the animals across the torrent. We still had five rivers to cross, with heavy rain also falling. After lunch in the inn we found we had another stream to cross, now a raging torrent. After waiting an hour we were able to get over. Fortunately we didn't have to cross it again, for when we next saw it, it was a terrible rushing flood with enormous muddy waves. A path skirted it along the edge of the fields so we got along safely, but we learned that just a short time after we passed a fresh flood came down and even those fields were inundated. Truly the Lord's special mercy.

The next morning the Hsi Shen Shan men heard that the bandits had already entered the city, just five li from their homes. They were anxious to start back. We talked with them about trusting the Lord, had a prayer meeting together, and they waited until the middle of the morning when the sky brightened and they started out. After going an hour or two, we had a terrific downpour. Soon an enormous roar of flood water came down the creek. One great tree was uprooted and as soon as the rain abated, the men began cutting it up for fear the next deluge would sweep it away. We would never have started out yesterday in such weather without the compulsion of the bandits. We were like the Israelites with the Red Sea before them and the Egyptian host behind. But the Lord made a way through the flood and we were full of praise.

We heard that mediators were dealing with the bandits with gifts and kind words, offering to supply what they wished. Meanwhile, it was good to see our friends again. We knew, however, that if the bandits came down this way we would have to cut short our visit and go home. We hoped this would not be necessary.

Though the situation didn't look good, we looked up and knew that the mercies of our Lord were still with us. We were just being careful to leave nothing undone which we ought to be doing.

As I look back I see that we were wonderfully led, so I was confident of further guidance. We heard that the very evening of the day we left Hsi Shen Shan in the rain, the bandits arrived there.

One might wonder why we didn't continue directly to Paotingfu then. But it continued to rain when we reached Liu Chia Chuang, continuing all night and the next day. At noon a terrific downpour caused a flood that made even the little creek in this valley impassable, not to mention the larger rivers farther down.

Sunday evening as we returned from a short walk at dusk we met the head of the Lai Yuan Tang Pu who was fleeing for his life. He reported that about 100 of the bandits were holding the city and seven or eight hundred were scattered over the villages, pillaging them and carrying off some of the women.

This didn't sound good so we tried to find mules to leave. While Mr. Liu trudged over the mountain to another village to try to find mules, we packed, then we dug out our books again and had our regular morning meeting.

Everyone had grown extra ears to hear all the reports, which of course were as various as possible. It was said that soldiers were blocking their way north and south, so the bandits must needs go east. And we were east! Others thought the bandits would keep to the main trails and not come into this out-of-the-way valley. However, that was uncertain.

We didn't feel overly anxious about ourselves. If they came, we could doubtless hide in the cornfields and keep out of their reach. But I felt concerned for my colleagues and family, all of whom would be much perturbed if they heard this news. To save others needless anxiety, it seemed we ought to leave if possible.

In the second place, it was probable our being here would draw the attention of the bandits and might make our host suffer at their hands. They, of course, were looking for just such prey as us. And the local non-Christians would certainly tell them of us in order to save their own skins if possible.

I couldn't forget that the "wicked fleeth when no man pursueth," but I preferred to get a head start! For the sake of the worried folk at the other end, I wanted to go if I could.

We contemplated hiking, but wading rivers up to one's waist was an impossibility, so we had to wait and see what the Lord had in store for us.

At noon, the sky finally cleared and the sun was on duty for the first time in days. It would make it easier for us to go but also easier for the bandits to come down. If we could just keep one jump ahead, all would be well.

The loving solicitude of our Christian friends and their willingness to go to all lengths for our safety and comfort was touching. I felt unworthy of such devotion.

The next afternoon Elder Lien arrived and, at the same time, news came that the bandits had departed for the north. He said none were left in Lai Yuan or the country district around there. This good news relieved the atmosphere and filled our hearts with praise.

So the Lord did answer prayer and gave us an opportunity to witness for Him there. That was good, indeed, for this was a place of great need and hungry hearts.

CHAPTER 30

BUT THAT WASN'T THE END (8-5-32)

"O give thanks unto the LORD; call upon His name;
make known His deeds among the people."
(Psalm 105:1).

Just as I typed my August 2 paragraph to assure those at home that it looked as though we could stay, the animals arrived to take us home. After much prayer and consultation it was decided we should leave. Elder Liu, after many sleepless nights, urged: "The magistrate has fled; there is no law; confusion reigns. You come here from so far away trusting us Christians. But the danger is too great. The communists already have many foreign missionaries in captivity, and if anything should happen to you, we are powerless."

Though the bandits had gone north, they were really nearer to us than when in the city. To get through to the north they would have to pass through a narrow winding gorge 40 li long. That was so that a handful of men could block their passage. If this happened—and it was said soldiers had been sent to do this very thing—then they would have to turn back and we would be right in their path.

Though reluctant to leave our unfinished task, the Lord said "Go," so we hastily packed up again, leaving our boxes with literature, medicines, and food supplies behind. Our escort consisted of three men with two strong mules and two good donkeys. I rode one of the latter and he proved a treasure, strong and steady without any bad tricks.

For the first 30 li riding was impossible and we had to clamber over rocks and jump from stone to stone crossing mountain rivulets. As we descended the mountain pass, we met two young men who accused us of being spies, saying if we couldn't give a good account of ourselves they wouldn't let us pass. However, they were satisfied and let us go unhindered, warning us that the Pao Hui T'uan or militia were just below and we had need to be cautious.

As we wearily stopped for a bit of lunch, we heard that another band of 1,500 bandits had gone up to Lai Yuan through the same southern pass, so that seemed to indicate that our decision to leave had been wise.

At the inn where we were to spend the night, we learned we had just missed the militia. We were grateful since they might have made things uncomfortable for us.

The farther we went, the larger the rivers and the hotter the weather. We were conscious that our way was being prepared by an unseen Hand. The second night was fearfully hot and the flies terrible. Under cover of darkness we went to the river where I performed some rather sketchy ablutions so I could change my perspiration-soured clothing, leaving my hair for another two days. I could appreciate now a little of the discomfort endured by so many during the terrible Boxer summer of 1900, but we were so grateful to be free such discomforts mattered not at all.

The inn where we stopped the third day wasn't really an inn at all, but just someone living near the food-shop, who had nothing better than a sort of chicken coop to offer us. Animals, packs, men all had to spend the night in the yard. The damp hole we had was much too small for four people, so my cot was put up in the yard and Miss Chao had a bed there too. While rain looked imminent, we had no place under cover to go, but we committed ourselves and our situation to our loving Father and went to sleep. During the night the sky cleared and morning found us with another dry, clear day for travel.

We inquired constantly to try to avoid the worst roads. Once we were told we couldn't possibly get to Paotingfu; all the country around there was simply a lake. We found actually that had been the condition two days before, but it had dried up sufficiently so it was possible to get through.

Before ten a.m., August 5, we were home in our beautiful compound we had left more than two months before. I must admit I got a terrible jar when I looked in the mirror. I looked like something the cat dragged home. My scales said 108 pounds but I think they stuck from the heat, and I had an appetite like a woodchopper.

The exquisite way the Lord makes things turn out just right was evidenced when suddenly in the middle of the night came a terrific downpour. If that had been the night before . . . but praise His name, it wasn't.

I recalled one morning on the road as I took down my mosquito net before dawn, a great scorpion fell on my arm. But like Paul of old, I shook off the deadly thing and felt no harm.

We did not know the fate of our friends throughout the country of Lai Yuan, but we were confident the Lord who directed every step of our way was also with them to comfort and protect. One day we shall know the full story and praise Him together.

If every authentic missionary must have a bandit story, this is mine. Wonderful, it seems to me, that I never laid eyes on a single bandit. Feeling we truly passed from death unto life, with grateful hearts we can only present anew our lives a living sacrifice to Him who is faithful and true, worthy of all adoration and praise.

Later: My bandit story got more exciting as the days went by! Mr. T'ien Feng Hsiang, the man who first brought news of the approach of the bandits, told me later the bandits started to follow us, but suddenly the creek flooded again so it was impassable and they couldn't get through! Just another detail of the perfection of His ways.

CHAPTER 31

BACK IN LIU CHIA CHUANG (10-20-32)

One day Miss P'an came to me in great distress. Someone had carried word to her home that she had gone crazy—simply because she repented during the meetings, confessing her sins and making restitution and presenting her life to the Lord. Her brother came down in haste to see her, and she was also expecting her uncle on the noon train. They said her mother hadn't eaten for three days, and they were all bemoaning that she would no longer earn money and support the family. Poor child, she was being counted worthy to bear the cross. We prayed together that the Lord would use her testimony at this time to win her whole family.

Later that day the chap who brought us home from the mountains turned up. He waited over until Monday to take us back.

So here we were, back in the very place from which we fled so precipitately in August. The weather had changed. Although there was a rather pale sun, it was cold enough for padded garments. But we had come well prepared with heavy things so we didn't mind.

We had a good trip. The Lord gave me two distinct blessings. One was that He took away my dislike for the mules. Many a time it had taken a great moral effort to get on one of the beasts. But this time I didn't mind them at all. There were many times when I had been in a state of worry and fret all the while I was on their backs, and terrified when they insisted on walking on the edge of nothing. But this time that fear was gone, and I didn't mind anything at all.

The other blessing was that I didn't get tired. Of course the cool weather helped. But it was still remarkable that I didn't tire. I am usually "laid out" after a day's ride, but this time, I was as chipper as possible at the end of the day.

When we reached Pei Kuan I made a flying visit to one of our Bible school students who hadn't gone back to school yet. She was the one whose father and mother died at the same time a couple years ago; her father's death was a suicide. Her uncle had tried to marry her off, but she absolutely refused. They now say they'll let her go back to school. May the Lord be gracious to the poor child. My visit was on the fly, because the mules kept going and I had to rush off to catch up with them, after a brief stop.

The only spots of color were patches of "burning bush" which are raised for brooms. They were brilliant.

To save time on the road the muleteers didn't want to stop for lunch, so we snatched a bite as we went. I would have liked a snap of myself hustling ahead of the mules munching sandwiches and raw tomatoes. I don't recommend this eating on the run for the best digestive action, but my doctors had fed me so much tonic that my ravenous appetite had to have plenty to appease it.

At night we followed our plan of cooking a big pot of thin rice. What was left over we warmed with hot water in the morning to sustain us when we started out.

The next morning we made an early start, getting on the road at 5:30. Though it was before dawn, a brilliant moon made light. We had to climb three mountains with the sketchiest of paths. Mules are certainly related to mountain goats. It was marvelous how they were able to dig their toes in and get along. But we got through without difficulty, though small parcels tied to our bedding rolls continually shook loose and had to be retrieved.

We reached Liu Chia Chuang about four p.m. Finding all well there, we looked expectantly for great things. Theatricals were to open soon, but God was able for even such distractions and we looked for great victories.

Though it was difficult to do anything constructive on the road I hoped to get a couple articles about the revival written: one for the *Chinese Recorder* published in Shanghai, and one for the *Life of Faith* in London. If it was His will He would make it possible. As I traveled I thought out some leads and then jotted them down when walking.

I remember the night we had the first fruit of our mission. One dear woman was deeply convicted of sin and confessed and prayed. I am inclined to believe that the failure of outsiders to come into the church indicates that the believers must first have a reviving.

My appetite continued to be tremendous. Never again would I be so foolish as to take tonic by the wholesale. Other times I had taken one teaspoon, but this time Dr. Mackey had prescribed two! Now I was suffering as a result.

The day before, our faithful God had done a new thing in our midst and many repented with tears. Dr. Sung had the habit each morning of asking the Lord for a promise from His Word. I had been following this plan with blessed results in my own heart as these promises always turned out to be significantly appropriate to the events of the day.

The promise for the preceding day was that God would bear witness with signs and wonders and divers miracles. This gave me faith to pray and by noon I could praise the Lord for that which my eyes had not seen. He first did a work in my own heart and showed me why I hadn't yet seen hearts melted. My own was too hard; I could preach the cross without tears. He sent the tears, and after the evening meeting we must have knelt in prayer an hour or more while one after another confessed their sins.

Elder Liu took the step of absolute surrender and obedience. He had a little store in his home and of course the heathen come to buy on Sunday as much as any other day. It was a strong temptation and for days it seemed he couldn't be freed. But praise the Lord, the night before he was delivered and determined to sell nothing on Sunday. What a testimony, and what power this purified church may exert.

Quite a few from other villages came to church. The devil beguiled some away to the theatricals, but we praised God for the faithful ones. A man driven by the demon of drink testified one night of great joy and real freedom. Praise the Lord who still works miracles.

CHAPTER 32

EVEN GREATER BLESSINGS (1-10-33)

My heart was ready to burst! Truly "His grace abounds more!" Earlier I told of passing from "death to life" in a miraculous escape from bandits. The months since have seen a spiritual fulfillment of the words which is an even greater miracle.

It began with the Bible conference in Paotingfu in October, a glorious time with the Bethel World-Wide Evangelistic Band, consisting of five young Chinese men and the leader Pastor Gih, who brought us much blessing last winter. Three of the group were gifted musicians and song leaders.

The teaching from the Bible was given by Pastor Gih and Dr. John Sung, who had a Ph.D. in chemistry from America. He gave up a brilliant life for the cross, to bring new life to tens of thousands.

The conference brought a deeper searching of heart and new experience of perfect submission, and my life has been different since. I found the Bible a new book, a personal message to me. From it my Lord each day gave a definite word of promise, which proved peculiarly fitted to the events and needs of that day.

For instance, after the conference we returned to the work in Lai Yuan which the bandits interrupted in the summer. We felt definitely led to return there, not knowing why. But we found the reason to be a cold and backslidden church. Prayer became a new thing as we were strained to pour out our hearts day and night for that place.

I felt I couldn't live unless the Lord used me to bring resurrection life to those dead ones. Then one morning God gave the promise: "God also bearing them witness, both with signs and wonders, and with divers miracles and gifts of the Holy Ghost, according to his own will" (Hebrews 2:4).

These words gave faith to believe we would see God working and, sure enough, that very day the Holy Spirit came in convicting power. With tears of penitence one after another confessed to God and cried for mercy. The elder—who was unwilling to keep the Lord's day holy, insisting he must keep his little store open and buy and sell—came to the place of complete surrender. It was glorious!

One poor man declared he couldn't give up his wine; he couldn't live a day without it. How securely the devil had bound him! As we cried to God for him, the Lord reminded me that He had commanded his disciples to cast out devils in His name. This gave me a new faith, and the fettered one was brought to believe and cry for deliverance. We used the blessed Name and the miracle was wrought.

The Lord's Word one morning concerned unwavering faith, and I had a presentiment something hard was coming. That very day a most promising lad rejected the Lord. Being fortified by the Word we were not cast down, but continued to believe he would yet be saved.

As moving time approached, news came that the bandits had returned. We were urged to wait until they passed by before going on to Wang Chia Chuang, but the Lord led us to go as planned, with the understanding we would leave whenever the danger became acute.

The menace continued the two weeks of our stay, but the Lord guided us with His eye. One night the news was especially disquieting, as it sounded as though the bandits were sure to come in our direction. The wealthy families under cover at night moved their valuables to hiding places in the hills, and we wondered what ought we to do?

That morning the Lord's promise was, "The beloved of the LORD shall dwell in safety by him, and the LORD shall cover him all the day long" (Deuteronomy 33:12). This assurance filled our hearts with peace and we happily remained at work.

The next day it did not surprise us to learn that the bandits had gone another route.

The mayor of this little community, one of the important men of the county, was well aware of the fact. Though we prayerfully gave him literature, the only result seemed to be long discourses on his own virtues. My verdict was "hopeless."

Then for several days the Lord's word concerned faith. "Ask of God - it shall be given." And we were given confidence to cry to God for this man. Wonder of wonders, he humbly confessed his sins and was willing to pray. A few days later he handed me a precious document in which he confessed his sins to God and testified to the Lord's saving grace with joy. His whole demeanor had changed.

Liquor had been his stumbling block; he couldn't overcome it. But when shown the Lord's saving power he later testified that it no longer had a pleasing odor and its power was broken.

Theatricals, which are always connected with idol worship, were scheduled to begin as soon as we left. But the responsible men were converted and canceled the engagement, to the great joy of the large crowd of girls who had given their hearts to the Lord. What a victory!

This was a definite fulfillment of the promise given when we went to Wang Chia Chuang: "Then will the LORD drive out all these nations from before you, and ye shall possess greater nations and mightier than yourselves" (Deuteronomy 11:23). We knew we were without any might of our own, but truly the Lord did drive out Satan and his powers from before us.

The Holy Spirit convicted one young woman of her tyrannical temper. She confessed humbly but the next day she was more wretched than ever. The trouble was that she had not apologized to her long-suffering family. When this was done, the joy of the Lord became hers. She later went to Bible school—the first to go from that great Lai Yuan country. We trusted she would later be useable in that needy place.

Great crowds attended the meetings in Hsi Pai Shan. The little church became thoroughly revived and outsiders were saved. After we left, the Holy Spirit continued to work: idols were torn from two temples and one sinning woman walked miles to find us and be helped to get rid of her burden of sin.

An elderly scholar in Hsieh Yi T'sun was familiar with the gospel, but obviously unsaved. I called, opening up the Word to him, but he felt sure he had no sin. The next day the Lord gave this word: "They overcame him by the blood of the Lamb, and by the word of their testimony" (Revelation 12:11). Being a typical Presbyterian I was unused to testifying, but a servant must obey, so I called again and told him my own experience. The Holy Spirit worked and another soul entered into the joy of the Lord.

Truly God's Word is living! How marvelous that God should speak thus to us who were but dust. The condition was absolute obedience. Many prejudices and habits had to go. For instance, I had always opposed women speaking on the street, but in one place the people were superstitious and afraid to come and listen. The Lord said, "Go to them!" so we did. God used the opportunity, and the joy of being workers together with Him was ours.

Late sleeping had been a lifelong habit. More than once I prayed and struggled against it, but in vain. Then our miracle-working Lord undertook for me, and all was changed without any effort on my part. I began to be awakened between four and five each morning and so had time to pray by name for each one of the scores who wrote me letters of testimony asking to be remembered. Truly He made all things new!

A new Bible, a new hunger and zest for prayer, a new faith that enabled me to see Him working miracles, a new joy in obedience, a new submission to the continual cleansing of the Holy Spirit, a new experience of deliverance from self: no wonder I had a new song in my heart! "Oh, magnify the LORD with me, and let us exalt his name together" (Psalm 34:3).

I began to read consecutively through the Bible, 11 chapters each day from the Old Testament and one from the New. One friend told me he read 11 chapters a day because there were 11 obedient disciples. That doesn't seem a very forceful reason, especially since I rather think Paul was added to fill up the number, but it was convenient to have a definite amount to read.

Someone asked me how I got my promises from the Lord. I just asked the Lord to speak to me from my daily reading and He caused a verse or a phrase to especially stand out and appeal to me. At the time I may not have seen its appropriateness, but before the day was over it had special significance. Sometimes the promise was really an admonition or a warning or a reminder of God's power. But always there was implied a promise to the obedient, and through the Word the Lord spoke with comfort and power to my own heart.

Girls of Florence's evangelistic band
(Florence far right)

CHAPTER 33

EVEN THE RAIN STOPPED (9-15-33)

There was a shout in my heart as I thought of the Lord's wondrous doings these past months. Almost under the shadow of the most ruthless bandit army that yet scourged North China, we were kept in perfect peace.

For months a summer trip to Lai Yuan had been in our prayers. June first we set out for vacation at a mountain camp halfway between Paotingfu and Lai Yuan. We carried supplies for the summer, hoping after a rest to itinerate. Though the news of irregular troops through the country was disquieting, the promises from God's Word were reassuring: Fear not; . . . believe . . . go and preach.

One day an invitation came to attend a summer Bible conference in Shanghai at Bethel Mission, but I had no intention of going if it were possible to start work. Then an elder from Lai Yuan asked us to postpone our trip for two weeks because of disturbed conditions. In waiting, we had the opportunity to attend the Shanghai conference.

First a day and a half by donkey (I was thrown off into the mud more than once). Then, packing in Paotingfu, torrents of rain turned the streets into deep rivers, so it looked as if I must wade to the train. But kind neighbors improvised a bridge with benches.

Such days of rich fellowship and spiritual refreshment at Bethel. This was the home base of the Bethel Band which brought such blessing to us last fall. In two-and-a-half years they saw 30,000 people enter into new life. Among these converts hundreds of volunteer evangelistic bands were formed. One new believer brought 120 people to Christ within a few months. When asked how he did it, he said, "I just tell them what the Lord did for me, and they want the same thing."

Personally I felt as though I might burst if I didn't get to preaching immediately. So when on the last day of the conference word came that my colleagues had been able to go up to Lai Yuan, I eagerly hurried back to join them. At Pukow when we were delayed hours by the train crew strike, it gave us a chance to talk to scores on the station platform. The crowd fairly fought for the tracts I had until the guards begged me to stop giving them out for fear of a disturbance.

The trip by mule into the mountains from Paotingfu was not too uncomfortable, though many dangerously swollen rivers had to be crossed. But the Lord's promise that morning was, "By faith they passed through the Red Sea as by dry land" (Hebrews 11:29). What confidence that gave, and it proved true. After two days' journey I reached T'a Yai Yi and went the length of the town distributing tracts and inviting people to an evening meeting.

And they came! For ten days we had great crowds every night, and sometimes passing troops also attended the service. Hundreds of men from remote hamlets had an opportunity to hear. It was impossible for us to reach all those places, but the Lord brought the people to us.

Many indicated they had repented, the most promising being a much respected man, the principal of the school. Following the meeting when we asked those who were in earnest to stay and learn to pray, the principal and a dozen others came, and proved very sincere.

Then one night spies brought word that a desperate horde of bandits was less than five miles away. Immediately the whole town went into a panic, everyone packing up and fleeing to the country. The blackness of night, mixed with wild rumors that the bandits had already arrived, filled the hours with terror. But what peace God gave. After prayer we decided not to leave. One by one the little group of Christian women and girls gathered in our room.

"This is heaven," they said. "We will stay with you."

Before we went to sleep several of us received the same promise: "God will make a way of escape." So early in the morning when five animals came to take our hostess to her farm two miles distant, the way seemed made for us to go along. Because the farm lay in an isolated valley, I wondered what possible good we could do there. But God had planned it and in nearby villages we found eager audiences. Scores we hadn't been able to reach in town had fled there and now had time to listen.

One night a tense whisper announced: "Eight renegade soldiers coming up the valley." Without stopping to gather up valuables, everyone stole noiselessly out the back gate and disappeared in the fields of corn and millet. It came so unexpectedly that we went out automatically. But as I prayed, hidden in a patch of flax, I became convinced that the Lord was just as able to save us in the house as in the field, so we returned and were not molested. Praise His name!

Though the day for departure brought a big rain and I supposed we would have an idle day of waiting, 17 men gathered from near and far intent on hearing the gospel. Many showed evidence of real faith, promising to read the little Testaments given them. So we thanked the Lord for these who would never have heard had we stayed in T'a Yai Yi.

The bandits looted within three miles of town, and then—wondrous answer to prayer—went another way, but they left a trail of suffering and distress: homes burned, old grandmothers tortured for their money, loved ones carried off for ransom, everything of value carried off or destroyed. Yet all believers in their path were miraculously kept from suffering and loss.

It was two days journey to our next place and the second day we were caught by heavy rain and took refuge in an inn. When the gray sky showed no sign of clearing, Miss Chao feared we might be delayed indefinitely. Then the Lord plainly told me, "Go out and witness in this place and the rain will stop." Though only three or four men stood at the big gate of the inn, as I began to preach folks sprang up from everywhere and a large crowd listened attentively to the gospel message. Need I add that the rain stopped?

I received a sermon from that rain. If we are yielded and usable, He can guide us not only with His eye but with His showers, and turn delays into thrilling opportunities. How glorious to be workers together with Him in His great plan. The will to be obedient brings freedom from all fear and anxiety. What a priceless treasure in these troublous times.

We were gone only a month, in constant peril from dangerous roads and lawless men, but the Lord preserved our goings. More people heard the gospel and more were blessed than on any former trip.

"Not unto us, O Lord, not unto us, but unto Thy Name give glory" (Psalm 115:1). Hallelujah, for the Lord our God, the Almighty, reigneth. Let us rejoice and be exceedingly glad, and let us give the glory unto Him!

CHAPTER 34

TEARING DOWN THE GODS (10-30-34)

The month of October 1934, as well as several months preceding, brought exciting new beginnings in many lives. Never was it more obvious that the work was all His. When a great river with dangerous rapids and quicksand had to be crossed after dark, His all-seeing eye led us unerringly. If some hard stubborn heart needed to be won, He laid an intolerable burden on our own hearts so we could but pray unceasingly until the victory came. He especially showed His power in bringing to repentance many who had been hindering the gospel.

Two of the women who graduated from Bible school in June decided to serve the Lord without pay. The fact that they attended school at all was a miracle, as their family opposed them and they had difficulty finding means to buy books and board. But they became real soul winners. One was not strong physically and solicitous friends warned her she could never stand the trip. But when she returned from the two months of strenuous travel everyone exclaimed "How well you look!" Indeed our God is able.

One young man avoided the meetings and I was impelled to talk to him on the street when we met. He insisted he had no sin so didn't need a savior and, indeed, felt satisfied the way he was. But his face belied his words and I spent much time in prayer for him. A few days later, deeply convicted of sin, he wrote to us, confessing his need—which I am sure the Lord met.

We next had the experience of going to a place where we were not wanted. The church member there had grown so cold he was about to give it all up. But in answer to prayer he received us and, while our stay was short, not a few turned to the

Lord. The mother of the family held out to the last, admitting it was good and true but wanting the family to believe without taking the step herself. Our hearts were greatly burdened for her. Just as we were packing up to leave she came and called upon the name of the Lord. What a victory! Her youngest daughter then enrolled in Bible school, another miracle which made us, like Paul, thank God and take courage.

In Liu Chia Chuang we were delighted to find many of the believers had been going on in the Lord and were full of His Spirit. The man delivered from drink two years ago was now a faithful witness. But while the believers had grown in Christlikeness, the unbelievers had grown desperately hard. We needed to pray they would yet accept the Saviour.

On our first visit earlier to Fan Chia Chuang the people acted timid and afraid. This time, however, we saw a great change; meetings were well-attended and a good group stayed to the Bible class. Our host was a man of influence in the community who had admired the gospel for years and wanted his son to be a Christian, but he himself was determined not to believe. Although we spent half the night prayerfully holding him up for salvation, he continued adamant.

How we cried to the Lord for him! The next morning as we were leaving, he came to say he had spent a restless night. He knew he must surrender to the Lord and wanted to do so before we left. With great rejoicing his family joined him in prayer. Many had been holding off, not daring to accept the Lord until this powerful kinsman did. Now that he had made his decision we expected a fine harvest in that little mountain valley.

In Nan Ch'eng Tze the meetings were well attended. The women at first seemed hopeless, bound by superstition and given over to worship false gods. But God broke down the barriers and many entered into the joy of the Lord.

Our hostess in the town of Nan Ch'eng Tze was a religious woman, her room fairly plastered with gods. She had been burning incense every evening without fail from the time she was 14, and laid up much merit by the repeating of Buddhist prayers. The gospel was a refreshing water to her thirsty soul, and she was irresistibly drawn to the crucified Saviour. Yet she feared the leaders of the false cult that had taught her so long. But finally, unable to resist longer, she came the last night to ask if she dared to tear down her gods. With great delight we consigned them to the flames, and the old lady called in other believers, saying, "Come and see where my gods are! Congratulate me!"

But the evil one doesn't let anyone escape without a struggle. She was tormented by fears, unable to sleep all night. In the morning she came, declaring she would have to go back to the old way. We stopped packing and united in desperate, believing prayer for complete deliverance from the evil one. She quieted, calling upon the Lord and her heart grew peaceful so she dropped to sleep. Only a miracle can keep her true, but we have a miracle-working God.

The enemy knows his time is short so he contested every victory. Many greatly used young evangelists were laid aside by sickness and we who knew how to pray began to lay hold of God for them that they would be raised up and used to save many more, also that these new believers would be kept under the precious blood, safe from every attack.

CHAPTER 35

HARVEST TIME (10-15-35)

Harvest time again! Meager in some places, but in the mountains we passed through fields rich with tall corn and heavy heads of millet. While the people gather in their treasure it is fitting that I give account of the spiritual harvest. One year before, six young women from the Bible school graduated and presented themselves to the Lord for country evangelistic work without salary. During the months they had gathered in precious sheaves.

We worked in bands, with younger and experienced workers in each group. Two or three times a year we came together for special meetings of praise and testimony.

The preaching of the cross is still the power of God to save from sin and the bondage of the evil one. One old woman steeled her heart against the gospel, refusing to pray with the others weeping before the Lord. No sooner did she return home than she was taken violently ill, after severe convulsions becoming stiff and cold. All the machinations of the witch doctor brought no relief. When it became evident they were powerless, the family sent for the evangelists. In answer to their prayers the sick one was immediately healed, calling on the Lord to save her. With her daughter-in-law, she turned from false gods to serve Him who is loving and true. Another old lady prayed the prayer of faith. Her cough was cured and her body, which had been weak and emaciated, was given new strength. Thereafter she led the band around to neighboring villages, a living testimony to the power of God.

The Lord can make even the wrath of man to praise Him, and a street fight was no exception. Two boys came to blows and one was literally "knocked cold." Life seemed extinct and no one in the excited crowd dared to touch the body flung in the dust of the street. They particularly feared because this boy's brother had lost his life in a similar brawl. Again the evangelists were called and they persuaded the father of the boy who had done the damage to carry the injured one into his home nearby. He and his wife had just repented when this sudden trouble descended upon them. The boy's death could mean endless lawsuits and feuds. They knelt with the evangelists on the dirt floor and prayed desperately. Within half an hour the lad's color returned and his breathing could be detected. He was soon able to say "Praise be to Jesus" but complained of pain in his chest. After further prayer this stopped and he was able to walk home by himself—but not before the two boys had made up their quarrel and gone off hand in hand!

One dear old lady, who will have a share in the great harvest, was an ardent worshiper of idols as was her father before her. She daily performed long ceremonies for making merit, spending all her money for incense and oil to burn a light before her gods. Then the Lord arranged an opening for the band to live in that home for a fortnight.

"Everyone else can be persuaded but the old lady is impossible," people told them. But after earnest prayer for many days the old lady tore down her gods with her own hands and consigned them to the flames. The daughter-in-law, who was supposed to be a believer, was still afraid to destroy the family god of wealth and the kitchen god. So the next night the old grandmother burned them up, too, determined to go the whole way with the Lord. Those whom she had formerly led to worship idols remonstrated with her for her change, but she answered, "I have now found the Truth; why don't you turn to the Saviour, too?"

Mrs. Liu had heard the gospel before the band visited her village, but she hadn't gotten rid of her burden of sin. She still followed the crowd and continued her idol worship. The clear preaching of a full salvation reached her weary heart, however, and she eagerly laid her sins at the foot of the cross. One of the first evidences of her new life was the courage and humility with which she went to a neighboring village and found an aunt with whom she had carried on a bitter feud for 15 years. She not only made peace with the older woman but brought her to hear the gospel and she, too, became saved. The gospel way of treating enemies still works!

The band planned to visit one place but the people who were supposed to receive them were decidedly inhospitable, frankly suggesting that they go elsewhere. But after prayer it was agreed that the evangelists should stop there. The Lord more than made up to them for this unpropitious beginning, for a large group of young men were thoroughly converted and immediately began to witness. They were among those asked to help with a big funeral. These new Christians asked to eat at a table by themselves; there they publicly asked a blessing and refused wine and tobacco.

One girl had a brilliant mind and noble spirit in a crippled body. A bad hip left her lame, so the active life of the bands seemed too strenuous for her. An urgent call came for her to teach school in a little country church and shepherd the flock. There she taught more than 30 children, from daylight to dark, leading adult Bible classes weekly and often daily, as well as Sunday services, and going out with groups of church members and school children to other villages to preach. Usually believers brought their carts to take her around, but when none were available, her brave spirit could not be vanquished and she walked, finding to her amazement that she could go miles. Truly she is an overcomer who will receive a crown!

Not only for the harvest did we thank the Lord. We were also thankful for each other, for the mutual love and helpfulness which filled our long strenuous days with song and laughter. With four people living in one small room, perhaps 10 by 12 feet, we got pretty close together. But being truly one in the Lord, there was no rubbing or friction!

Usually two members of the band work the outlying villages while two take the home meetings, all coming together at meals. Results are eagerly reported and each victory and defeat taken unitedly to the Lord, looking to the Great Commander to direct the next attack. For it was spiritual warfare we were engaged upon, and hosts of spiritual wickedness must be overcome. If things were going badly, we let the meeting go and took time out to pray. We know where the victory must be won.

At that time our band chose a new name—Ling Chan Pu Tao T'uan. Literally it means "Spiritual Warfare Evangelistic Band," but for short, we called it in English "The Battle Band." We planned to keep up the attack until He comes who will gain the final victory with the majesty of His presence.

Farewell to Florence on return to U.S.
Spiritual Warfare Evangelistic Band 1936
(Florence in front row, right center)

CHAPTER 36

THE WORK CONTINUES (2-1-36)

Is there any thrill equal to that of seeing the Holy Spirit work in hearts? After giving a simple gospel message what joy it was to have a dignified country gentleman come up and say: "Please help me to pray. I want to ask Jesus to forgive every sin of the past 39 years. I want to commit myself to Him to be kept from ever falling into sin again."

The Lord had greater things to show us: on the closing night of the campaign a whole roomful knelt in prayer. All had a slip of paper in their hands on which they had written out their sin account. They wanted to make the transaction clear and definite, so each read out in a clear voice the record of their own guilt and begged a merciful Saviour to blot it all out.

The big market town of Hsia Shou was shaken. Truly "The people that sat in darkness [saw] a great light" (Isaiah 9:2). Many of the most active opponents became eager inquirers. At their importunity we rearranged our schedule in order to go back for three more meetings the next week.

Crowds kept coming, in spite of two fierce dogs that greeted everyone ferociously.

While there we discovered that Hsia Shou had a Good Samaritan, Mr. Lu. One day on the way to town he found a man lying in the road almost dead from exposure. Not without reason many wary ones passed by on the other side, for frequently a would-be benefactor could end up entangled in endless blame and trouble for his pains. But the love of Christ constrained Mr. Lu to investigate. The man, who lived in a village eight miles away, took sick at work and after some days was urged to go home. He started but could go no farther. Mr. Lu helped the fellow to his feet and half-carried him to Hsia Shou, where, seeing his death-like appearance, no inn would receive him. Finally Mr. Lu found a place where he could buy hot food for him. While the sick man ate, the Good Samaritan hurried home and, without consulting anyone, hitched up the family cart to take the friendless one to his destination.

As soon as his purpose was known, everyone was apprehensive. "You don't know what ruse he may be playing. Is he telling the truth? Look at him. He'll die on the way and then see the trouble you'll be in with a dead man on your hands!" But the intrepid Samaritan quietly took the man to the police station, registered his name and address, and signed up indicating his intention of taking him home. If he died en route the police could testify he had been in a dying condition when they started. But the Lord answered prayer, and the man was safely delivered to his home. When he gratefully asked his benefactor's name he was told: "Just thank the Lord Jesus; He had mercy upon you." In those days it was dangerous to be on the road after dark, but the Good Samaritan was kept safe from all harm all the way home.

CHAPTER 37
BACK IN CHINA (2-17-38)

After a separation of five months my trunks finally arrived. I parted from them in Yokohama in August, expecting to pick them up the following week, but by mistake they were put on a "round-the-world" boat and went as far as Suez before they were halted and started back. Meanwhile I have lived out of a week-end case filled with voile dresses and hot-weather accessories.

Fortunately the weather continued warm until I reached North China in October, when I speedily acquired a wardrobe of padded and fur-lined Chinese garments which kept me comfortable. I never dreamed I could be separated from all my worldly possessions and miss them so little.

It was one of the Lord's miracles that in spite of the disturbed conditions they actually did arrive. What an exciting day that was. All the girls of the band came to witness the opening. I felt like the father of the prodigal son calling in his friends to rejoice with him over the wanderer's return. The girls rejoiced over all the things that would be useful in our work.

The whistling teakettle, the earphone for the deaf, and scores of other things were immediately put to use. We all joined in thanking the givers in America and the loving heavenly Father who brought them safely to us.

I spent a happy month in Peking. But the dictionary doesn't seem to have a word to express how I felt in getting back to Paotingfu and joining the dear ones who showed such heroic fortitude and were so miraculously preserved through the bombardment here. Probably 5,000 people were huddled together in our buildings at the time of the attack. Scores of shells fell within the compound. Some of the buildings were seriously damaged, but only eight lives were lost; these were all refugees, not members of our staff.

When I arrived six weeks later, the worst of the debris had been cleared away but many yawning holes bore mute testimony to past peril. It seemed a miracle that there were not hundreds of casualties. With several others I made the trip down from Peking in a boxcar of a troop train. The train left the station some miles from the city and we had to make many trips back and forth before we finally were permitted to depart.

As we bumped along I almost wept with gratitude that I was again permitted to see our North China countryside. Fortunately, darkness masked the compound when we arrived so we were not shocked by the war scars. All the buildings were windowless. The panes in our living rooms were pasted over with paper to keep out the cold wind. Having heard that nothing could be bought in our once prosperous city, we brought some glass with us and other supplies. Under the skillful direction of our mission architect the major damage was speedily repaired, enabling us to present an almost normal appearance.

This could not be said for the city, however. It was still a pathetic picture of desolation, even though thousands of people had returned.

About 700 refugees on the compound were camped in a most primitive fashion in all available buildings. They had already organized into study classes and were being daily taught the gospel. The terrific experiences they had been through seemed to soften their hearts and not a few were truly converted. Out of the fiery trial many Christians also received definite spiritual blessing.

We rejoiced to work with this large group within our gates, and on November 22 we were able to open a girls Bible Institute with an enrollment of more than 100 students and offering a varied curriculum. A little later some of the country districts became unsafe for young girls so we invited the daughters of church members to come in, providing them with two meals of millet daily. Those who could afford to pay had a noon meal also.

In this way an interesting group was brought together. Most were exceedingly keen to study and considered this the chance of their lives. We were happy to give them this haven for physical growth. Because it was impossible to itinerate in the country now, I was glad to head up this Bible school work and try to give these girls the best possible training. The boys' Bible school started about a week later than the girls; about 50 were enrolled, the most we have ever had. The next week we then began a house-to-house campaign in the city, giving a gospel message in every home. The present distress was a fruitful time for personal work.

We were amazed at the fortitude with which people picked up the shattered fragments of their lives and homes and cheerfully started on again. The small sum available for relief helped, but it couldn't touch the fringe of the misery around us. It became more acute as spring advanced. Our usual big station family of sixteen missionaries was depleted by many being in America on furlough and others being detained in Peking by illness, so we were only six and part of the time seven. This meant everyone had to double up on jobs. My share was station secretary, station treasurer, and Bible school principal, in addition to my usual evangelistic work, plus we all shared in the load for the relief work.

Christmas season was a blessed time. We exchanged no individual gifts but had great joy making Christmas real to the hundreds of refugees within our gates. The early morning singing, lighted trees, and special meetings made a deep impression on those who were having their first Christmas. Each refugee received a treat of a pound of white steamed bread, with candy and peanuts for the children.

However, losses of the common people by destruction and looting were past computation. We had been administering relief ever since the bombing, giving grain, warm clothes, and bedding to many who lost everything. The hospital daily received new cases of civilians who had been wounded in guerrilla warfare. They had room for only the most needy ones. Usually some patient had to be persuaded to go home before a new case could be admitted.

We were so grateful to the Lord for permitting us to be here to help in this time of appalling need that every day was Thanksgiving Day with us. One band of our girls was cut off in the mountains and unable to get back to Paotingfu, but the Lord used them to bring a great reviving to the little church there.

We praised the God who triumphs in spite of everything, and we believe He prepared praying friends at home for such a day as this.

CHAPTER 38

RAIDS AND REFUGEES, BUT THE WORK GOES ON (6-1-38)

The weeks were simply hurtling through space, almost as though running away from the suffering and distress they were loathe to witness. But the Lord's mercies continued in the midst of man's inhumanity to man, and His faithfulness shone brightest when the clouds were blackest.

The Chinese New Year brought a time of special prayer, and we noted the Christ-like spirit of General Chiang Kai-shek's proclamations. We gave thanks for the humane treatment of prisoners and the religious liberty for schools, two glorious things amid the chaos.

For several weeks after Chinese New Year, a dozen of us went daily into the city for house visitation and chapel preaching, our first experience going door-to-door. We almost invariably obtained a hearing and many hungry hearts were found. The Christian calendars we presented to each household were eagerly received, as were the tracts and gospels. Not a few tore down idols and joined in prayer as soon as they heard the good news. As a result, many new inquirers were enrolled in daily chapel services at the city church, continuing to attend Sunday services.

Scarcely had we covered half the city when a fresh influx of refugees required all our time. Pathetic, having just escaped from their burning villages, they had been through weeks of sleepless nights followed by the terror of flight. Loss of home and loved ones had left them stunned. Many were from wealthy families, but all looked haggard and worn. We had no luxury to offer them—just a bit of straw and a mat on a brick floor with millet porridge to eat. Even with us, their night's rest was frequently broken by the rattle and bang of firing, but they felt safe and expressed their gratitude. Gradually, as their minds opened to the comfort of the gospel, many became new creatures spiritually as well as physically.

This time we did not permit the refugees to do their own cooking, but insisted they buy their porridge from the common kitchen. Destitute ones were fed from funds given by friends. This arrangement enabled us to improve sanitary conditions and gave the women time for study. For a time we had to open an additional dormitory each day to accommodate newcomers, but finally the inflow decreased and we were able to manage.

Many of our country Christians were among the refugees and came expecting spiritual refreshment. We couldn't disappoint them so had special meetings for them while evangelistic services were held for unbelievers. The children and mothers with babies also had separate gatherings. With opportunities for personal interviews and prayer, many found new life.

In the spring the Bible Institute grew by leaps and bounds. When the boys reached an enrollment of 70 or 80, the housing problem became acute and some had to sleep in a basement. In the girls' school with almost 300 girls, I felt like the old lady who lived in the shoe. We had to continually contrive and shift until every inch of space was brought to highest usefulness. Half of the girls slept on the floor, and the porches bulged with them. To conserve space many of them ate their meals standing up. Most ate only two meals a day. They had millet porridge for breakfast, then took turns pushing the grindstone to prepare the kaoliang flour which was made into black steamed bread for their supper. This, with a bit of pickle or vegetable, was all they had, but they were thankful for even this much since many people in the country now had nothing but chaff and weeds.

One group of girls had a terrifying time escaping from soldiers. They had heard vaguely of me and came in desperation as a last hope. Some had had their homes looted and burned;

others had lost the breadwinner of the family. I rejoiced that the little gifts from Sunday schools and individuals the year before made it possible for me to take in these penniless ones.

Many of these girls had to stay with us throughout the summer, so we planned a six week's summer vacation, specializing in music and sewing. I didn't know how they would be fed, but Elijah's God was our God. "The barrel of meal wasted not, neither did the cruse of oil fail" (1 Kings 17:16).

As a basis for an appeal to the Red Cross for relief funds, we made a survey of our field and 17,000 families were reported to be without food as a result of having their crops destroyed and homes looted or burned. Not nearly enough funds came in to meet this need. The most our relief committee could do was to hand out day by day little doles of grain and cash to a few of the most desperate who appealed to us. About 150 special cases were fed on the compound.

One family was kept from starvation by weaving coarse country cloth and selling it to us. This we used to make countless quilts to loan to the refugees. That spring we also made 100 flyswatters. All the kiddies on the compound came into affluence through being paid 10 coppers per hundred for their catches. Who would like to buy a dollar's worth of flies? We could give you 17,756 for that price. When I realized how these would have multiplied by midsummer, I counted it money well spent.

Repeated raids in the neighborhood and a pitched battle under our eaves brought in another flood of refugees. They filled the evangelistic tent, a large basement, and the whole church, spending the nights with us and going home days. Each evening we held meetings for them.

That spring I turned farmer. Much of the garden space on the compound was going to waste and some of our country Christians had nothing to do, so we put the two together and produced enough vegetables to supply most of our large compound family.

It was impossible to plan for anything that year. Our work was thrust upon us from day to day, and we just tried to be ready for the Lord's use in each situation.

We had many precious experiences of the Lord's planning and provision. In the midst of so much that was terrible our hearts were filled with singing. We had wonderful fellowship with our Chinese colleagues, and the girls of the Evangelistic Band did valiant service in the school and among the refugees.

I knew the prayers of many were responsible for our well-being during those months, and I prayed that each intercessor would share the joy of the Lord that was ours. Apart from Him we could not continue a single hour.

CHAPTER 39

THE SPIRIT-FILLED LIFE (9-26-38)

On September 26 the Lord sent His servant Pastor Wong Chao Hsiang to Paotingfu. Though a week ahead of schedule, it was the Lord's time and all worked out to His glory.

That day a mundane matter delayed my starting to the city—a hole in my stocking! I wondered as I started out if the Lord had some purpose in such a trivial hindrance. Halfway down the drive I met Pastor Wong coming in, and knew the Lord had delayed me that I might be present to receive him and get him settled. What a God we have! With all His infinite greatness He still concerns Himself with the minutest matters.

That evening, after the leaders came in for prayer, Pastor Wong explained simply that in coming to Paotingfu he had felt that a revival of prayer was the thing most needed. All our hearts echoed an "Amen."

Messengers were sent out the next morning to the country churches within reach urging the leaders to come at once to share the feast with us. The alacrity with which they responded indicated the hunger in their hearts. Soon we had a good representation from all but the more distant places.

Pastor Wong spent several hours morning and afternoon meeting with individuals and groups for prayer. Elder Chao, the principal of the Girls' Bible School, was one of the first upon whom the Spirit was poured out. He surrendered a root of bitterness, wrote a letter of apology, and his heart was filled with hallelujahs. He felt led to ask Pastor Wong to bring a simple message from Ezekiel, chapter 44, where two types of Levites are mentioned: those who could not approach God but could only keep busy in the outer court serving people, and the second type who had access to the very presence of God and served Him without burden or sweat. How we longed to be numbered in that holy company. In the time of prayer the Lord Himself drew near and tears gave place to joy.

As the meetings went on, the work didn't seem to be quite deep enough. Then Sunday night, October 2, there came a dream. It seemed I was starting on a trip and scolded my companion for not having her things packed. But I soon found out I was not ready either and had a great scramble getting things sorted. During this process I again scolded my companion for standing in my way and hindering my packing. But my own conscience rebuked me for I had stood around and hindered her when she was trying to get ready.

This little dream startled me. Could it be possible I was not ready for the spiritual blessing for which we longed? And was I hindering others? In my morning reading I felt directed to Isaiah 32. There it speaks of a year of barrenness and urges humility on the careless women. This went home, too, for it did seem the year had been pretty barren. Could it be possible there was carelessness about small matters? The Spirit of Truth brought to mind certain things.

Since the exhortation was in plural it seemed to fit us as an evangelistic band, so I called the girls together and we spent the hour before the morning meeting in Bible study and prayer. I told them what the Lord had shown me. But an hour was not enough, so after the meeting we went back to our upper room and the Lord spoke to us, each one. So many little things were confessed and forgiven, while tears turned to laughter as the Spirit was poured out upon us. As we prayed through, it was a glorious experience. At the same time other groups were also praying.

In one room four men were on their knees pouring out their hearts when they were aware of the opening of the door and another figure kneeling beside them. They had great liberty in prayer, and as they prayed around they waited for the latecomer to lead. He did not speak so they looked up—and they were alone. Their hearts were filled with holy awe and exaltation as they found that each had had the same distinct impression. Their Lord had truly presenced Himself in their midst.

Lessons on prayer—plus prayer at midnight, at dawn, at sunrise and at noon—were full of help. Lessons on Christian unity struck deep and resulted in the Presbyterian and Pentecostal groups joining their evangelistic efforts and prayer meetings. Truly the Lord's work was greatly strengthened thereby.

One of Pastor Wong's striking expressions was "po li tu tze"—stomach of glass, indicative of absolute transparency, nothing hidden. This was necessary to preserve our unity and to keep little devisive things from creeping in.

Pastor Wong was a Southern Methodist, a graduate of Nanking Theological Seminary. While frequently dissatisfied with his own spiritual state he passed unmoved through many revivals. Finally a single word went to his heart with power: "If any man thirst, let him come unto me, and drink" (John 7:37). As he sat in the meeting, the Holy Spirit came upon him in mighty power. He was filled with hilarious joy and immediately began to witness at home and abroad. His wayward son was saved; his home which had caused him much distress became a bit of heaven. He witnessed in his old seminary and the professors concluded that he was mentally unbalanced. But when he preached in the church, other dry, dead pastors were moved to tears and received new life. Though he had the outer witness of the Spirit, there were still areas of his inner life to be brought under subjection to the Spirit. Spiritual pride, impatience, a critical spirit—these were taken away as he matured in the life wholly lived in the Spirit. He was miraculously healed of serious digestive trouble. Gradually he was led to leave his pastoral work to minister to the church at large. The Lord used this servant to bring reviving and especially to heal the schisms and divisions in His body.

Four questions need to be answered as we seek to live the Spirit-filled life:

Is this God's will?
Is it God's will for me?
Is this God's time?
Is this His way?

We were beginning to have more of a real heart concern for every member and every part of His body. One morning we were led to pray for the church in Such'uan, that the Lord would send men of His choosing to revive it. That noon word came of the proposed visit of Edwin Orr and Andrew Gih to that area.

Though the adversary was busy, our eyes continued on our triumphant Lord.

Florence and sister Lorna, front, left to right,
with evangelistic band, upon Lorna's visit to China in 1938

CHAPTER 40

HARVEST AT LAST (9-1-38)

At last—harvest! In our west field God mercifully gave an abundant crop. Half-starved folk forgot their weakness and suffering in the joy of gathering in the new grain. God had given, and I prayed that the wickedness of men would not take away this precious food supply.

To the east of us, dikes were broken for military purposes so the fields were flooded and there was nothing to harvest. The past year the crops were largely destroyed during the fighting, so this was the second year of famine for them.

In these last hungry weeks before harvest we stretched every nerve to give relief—just a wee bit here and there to someway sustain life until the longed-for new grain ripened. It was a heartbreaking business to pick the most desperate from among so many needy ones. We spent every cent of our grant from the relief committee; in fact we went several hundred dollars in the red, but little gifts here and there wiped that out. I was sure the givers were glad to know their help came in time to meet this emergency. The local church raised a fund particularly to aid their Christian brethren in the country. Now we turned our energies to doing something for the flooded area, and we prayed that no further disaster increased the number needing relief.

Insufficient food had so lowered people's resistance that there was a tremendous amount of sickness: dysentery, malaria, typhoid, and now cholera. The hospital stretched its capacity to give free beds to the poor. But, even so, only a small proportion of the cases could be taken in. It was pure joy to slip a dollar here and there to some sick one who had no appetite for the coarse fare of semi-famine conditions. How they longed for some rice gruel or white flower noodles. One didn't like to think of the multitudes denied even this small comfort.

The city health department asked the hospital to co-operate in giving free cholera inoculations, and nearly 6,000 were done in three afternoons. We evangelistic workers caught them "before and after" with the gospel. As they lined up in front of the hospital, we went along giving out tracts and brief messages. Then near the hospital exit we had some benches in the shade where many stopped to rest and listen a while before going home. Officially we were supposed to care only for the people of the west suburb. But hundreds came from the city, too, preferring to get their treatment from us. Such confidence was gratifying. They loyally maintained that our inoculations were painless!

In June we closed the porridge kitchen and sent the refugees home, with a little grain or money to help them along. We continued to help some of the war widows, however, and a few stayed on to sew for us. One new industry was the making of American flags. Our property had to be marked with these, and a terrific windstorm blew the old ones to tatters. The women made the beautiful flags all by hand, and it was a heap of work. Imagine sewing 48 stars on both sides of a field of blue!

I took special interest in the sewing. The girls made handkerchiefs, shoes, and summer and winter garments. Many of them had no change of clothes. One can hardly imagine what that meant in weather that kept one dripping with perspiration, so we conspired to give them the garments they had made. I gave the word to have them distributed. It seemed less than five minutes later that a flock of youngsters stood at my door with beaming faces and fresh new clothes!

After two weeks of vacation a new term began. The winter before, we provided simple food for many girls whose homes were unsafe or impoverished. Many of these girls proved to be good material. To help them further, we decided that scholarship aid would be given on a merit basis. We found eight girls whose character, deportment, and scholarship classed them as honor students, and paid their food and fees.

I must report the success of the flyswatting campaign. We spent about $10 in American money and killed 792,760 flies! As a result we were practically fly-less in what was usually the worst season. For a long time we burned great piles of flies every day and still seemed to make no impression on them. I nearly lost hope. But perseverance won, and we were so thankful to be free of the pests. It meant more for the health of the compound than many inoculations, and a lot of hungry children made lunch money for themselves by means of the flyswatter.

In June it was my great joy to have my sister visit me. Unless one has lived long in a foreign land far from home, one can hardly imagine the special thrill of being able to introduce one of your very own to the strange sights and scenes among which you live. It surely was a dream come true.

Every detail of the visit was perfect. The weather was cool and pleasant. I met her at Tangku and we came at once to Paotingfu for five days, where she saw our war-scarred home and met my dear colleagues and friends. They couldn't do enough to honor her, so we feasted early and late. All were eager to hear of her work among the Chinese in the Chinatown section of San Francisco where she headed the Donaldina Cameron House, a Presbyterian mission.

Later we visited Peking for 10 wonderful days among its temples and palaces and shops. It was such fun to visit them all again with her. Some were marvelously beautiful, having just been renovated the past year before the trouble. We visited the Summer Palace, and reveled in this glimpse into a great past with its promise of a still greater future.

Shopping was particularly fascinating because of the state of exchange. Even quite a flat pocketbook could stand a beautiful new coat and a few other souvenirs of this ancient land. A day with friends in Tientsin, and then I saw her on her boat at Tangku again.

We hoped that as soon as the harvest was over we could scatter to the country. We knew there would be new situations and new problems, and we would need as never before wisdom and grace from above.

Chapter 41

Workers Together With God
(5-20-39)

"Workers together with God." Do you catch the picture? I see a wee fellow sitting with his daddy at the wheel of a powerful machine: the father is driving, but he permits the little chap to put his hands on the wheel, too, and the child's eyes glow with the exhilaration of accomplishment.

These past months our heavenly Father had permitted us to put our hands on the wheel of His great purposes and we were thrilled with the glorious results.

God had been working in the hearts of unbelievers, preparing them to receive the gospel. In nine weeks we lived in six villages and preached in twenty more. In practically every one some wanted to repent at the first hearing of the good news. Almost without exception these outside villages begged us to come stay and teach them further. We could not accept these invitations as our schedule was made out for months ahead; the continued importunate pleading simply wrung our hearts.

In one village a thriving church had already sprung up, and we preached on the streets there several times. The young men began to attend our classes in a neighboring village each evening. In those days few people dared venture from their homes after dark, and to travel to another village at night was almost unheard of, but they did so as long as we remained in that district.

The women then began to come to our study class in the daytime, walking a mile or two each way, usually carrying a baby. A number of them mastered the phonetic. Scores were clearly converted. The head of the village with his whole family turned to the Lord. He prepared a room for church services and we took turns leading meetings there each Sunday after-noon. Every service saw new conversions.

On the last Sunday, two special trophies of grace were brought to the Lord. An old woman and a younger man had followed their parents in a religious sect. They were concerned lest their departed elders be offended by the renouncing of their faith. When their minds were set at rest on that point, they gratefully laid their burdens down at the feet of the Saviour.

Such crowds of eager new believers created a Bible fam-ine. Evidently similar conditions prevailed all over China and the presses could not print Bibles fast enough. I early exhausted the entire Paotingfu supply and kept pleading for more—"Any-thing just so it is a Bible." They were sent out to me as fast as they arrived but always not enough. I needed at least 100 more to satisfy those awaiting them.

And gospel posters! Every supply that came created a near riot. Pictures of the life of the Lord and posters with a large cross were in greatest favor. In all my experience I had never been "cleaned out" like that before.

On our last moving day two carts came after us and our baggage. One was an ox cart. Two of us rode our wheels and preached in two villages en route. Though it was a busy morn-ing, great crowds gathered to listen closely. Even the usually rowdy children were quiet and orderly. We felt the seed fell on good soil. Everyone wanted to learn to pray.

We reached our destination in the heat of noon but they left their dinners and came to hear anyway, eager for the Bread of Life. We thanked the Lord for our wheels which saved those precious hours on the road and enabled us to reach two ne-glected villages as well.

During these nine weeks our one little band recorded the names of 450 new believers; doubtless there were as many more whose names we could not learn. But the 450 were practically all "hand-picked fruit" who were helped individually to repent and confess. We would have to wait until we gathered home the next month to hear the reports of the other three bands.

A temple fair in Yan Ch'eng brought a golden opportunity for three days. These annual fairs are the only chance the country people have to buy implements, household utensils, and so on. They are also great social events with much visiting and playing. Usually there are theatricals to entertain the crowd. This year there were no theatricals, but there was a gospel team and the crowd listened to the preaching all day long. Spring winds kept the dust in constant motion so the preachers came home day after day looking like dusty idols.

One day there was a panic, the mob stampeding in terror, fleeing for their lives. As nothing happened, in a little while they came drifting back.

On the third day, the great open square seemed practically deserted, but as soon as we started to sing, everyone gathered around us so we did "business as usual" although the dispensers of other commodities had few customers. For days after the fair people kept hunting us up: they heard and believed and wanted help in making their peace with God.

Countless idols were torn down and burned. When we moved to one place we noted a piece of plain white paper over the stove in about the position usually occupied by the kitchen god. On investigation we found this was a bit of camouflage to try to keep both the god and us from being offended. Our hostess knew we wouldn't be pleased to see him there, but she didn't dare to dislodge him. So she compromised by neatly covering him up. However, the second day she was delivered from fear and boldly tore him down. The day we left, a god of wealth neatly hidden away was also destroyed.

In this home the son was pathetically bound by gambling, drinking, and temper. He had the best intentions in the world but simply couldn't break with sin. Again the Lord reminded me that He sent forth his disciples giving them power to cast out demons, so the all-powerful name of Jesus was invoked and the poor slave set free. How we praised such a Saviour!

One woman was possessed of a demon that had tormented her mother-in-law before her. The family was given over to demon worship. Regularly on the days of the new and full moon the woman would be thrown into a coma which sometimes lasted several days. She turned to the Lord but did not dare to tear down all her idols as her husband still worshiped them. During her next attack the evangelists came to the home. The husband was converted, closed up his gambling joint, the gods were torn down, and the woman was delivered through prayer. Thereafter she had a wonderfully happy testimony.

God's wondrous working was seen especially in the way He cared for His own and led them in the path of faith. We had been out less than a month when that which we feared came upon us. The city was taken and, from that day, the people's lives were a nightmare of dread and suffering.

It happened on a Sunday. I had led the morning church service in the city and afterwards went to a nearby village for an afternoon meeting. Soon the big shells began to explode very near us, and the house shook with the concussions. Then a great joy filled my heart as I reminded the others that the next shot might send us into the very presence of our blessed Lord! But He willed it otherwise. I took advantage of a lull to return to the village where we were living. On the way I met the stretcher-bearers with their pathetically still burdens, and my soul was filled with overwhelming hatred of the whole ghastly business of war.

One day a mother sought me in great distress. Her son had been taken. Would I find a way to secure his release? I assured her no human means could be relied upon, but we could commit the matter to the Lord. We prayed for the young man, not only for his deliverance but that this trouble might bring him to repentance. A few minutes later the mother again pleaded, "Think up some plan for me; what should I do?"

"Do? It is already done," I assured her.

"I don't need to do anything else? Shall I just go home?"

"Certainly; just give the Lord an opportunity to work." The next day she came back beaming.

"Just look at me," she cried. "I had scarcely gotten home yesterday when my son returned safely."

Several times when a whole village fled in terror, a large number took refuge with us and we were able to introduce them to the One who is a hiding place from the storm.

God worked in the hearts of believers giving them a deep sense of sin. I have never seen such humble contrition, such genuine loathing of sin. We praised the Lord for His cleansing blood and the power of the Spirit.

"Pray ye the Lord of the harvest." He answers when we give Him the slightest chance. As we faced the spring work our numbers seemed pathetically inadequate. Then God put the burden for souls on three new graduates and we joyfully added them to our band. Just then a letter came: "The Lord wants me to send you this check. I don't know why." But we knew why; it was the expense money for the new graduates.

When in the country, I felt handicapped by lack of workers. Meetings for outsiders, classes for believers, and children's work kept us tied down so we couldn't reach the surrounding villages. Then one of our married girls unexpectedly joined us, having felt led to come and help for a month or two. She brought us home mail, including a letter that opened: "I feel impelled by the Spirit to send you my tithe this month." And there was the provision for her needs! The Lord of the harvest had worked at both ends, preparing the heart of the worker to answer His call and moving His faithful stewards to provide the laborer's hire.

With these additions, we formed four bands and planned itineraries in four counties. Even so, we had to refuse many urgent invitations. An older man came one day: "We never knew what it was to be saved until one of your Bible school girls came and told us. Now hundreds of people come every day longing to hear, but we don't know how to teach them. Can't you send us someone?" That was the plea and we needed to answer speedily while we could for the gospel door already had been slammed shut in two counties, and we needed to buy up every opportunity that remained and to "pray the Lord of the harvest."

There was great need for relief work in certain parts of the field and it was being heroically carried on. During the vacation, one young teacher went down to manage some relief in a stricken area. The arrangement to transfer the money fell through so he came back without having accomplished much. At that time there was considerable fighting in that area so we were thankful that he returned safely. But the next day he said, "I could not sleep last night for thinking of those poor people. I must go back and carry the money to them." That was a dangerous proceeding, he well knew, but he said, "I can no longer live with myself; I must live for others." The Lord was with him and he fulfilled his errand of mercy without mishap.

Day after day, we didn't know what lay ahead for us. There was no flour to be had; millet and other grains were twice the normal price. A dry hot spring augured ill for the wheat crop. But we knew Who was ahead of us. Our God was leading on through untried ways, and all we needed was grace to trust Him fully. For those who prayed, their hands, too, were on the wheel. It was thrilling!

CHAPTER 42

FLOODS AND TESTIMONIES (9-20-39)

"Yet I will rejoice in the LORD,
I will joy in the God of my salvation"
Habakkuk 3:18

So sang the prophet of old in the face of disaster. That same note of praise filled our hearts in spite of overwhelming calamities. The principal of a Bible seminary in flood-stricken Tientsin wrote, "We are determined to trust His grace when we cannot trace His ways." We did not know what blessing there could be in this bitter cup of suffering; but we knew we had a loving heavenly Father and that was enough.

The spring drought broke on the fourth of July. A few days later floods came roaring down from the mountains, spreading death and devastation. Houses and fields alike were carried off by the waters and sometimes their owners, too. Those who escaped found themselves left with patches of stones washed clean of every bit of soil. Farther down, as the torrents passed over fertile fields, they dropped a deep layer of sand, burying the soil along with the farmer's hopes. Still farther down, the water collected in great seas. Thousands of homes were undermined and sunk in the flood. Refugees camped precariously on banks or else fled. The police prevented their congregating in the city, but they were everywhere. Grain tickets were distributed with the result that we foreigners were almost mobbed by pleading women when we stepped out of our gate.

The plight of these people was heart-rending and one didn't dare think of the prospect of a North China winter. We started a porridge kitchen in one watery oasis. By stern elimination the number was kept down to 800, a fraction of the hungry ones. Even so, available supplies only sufficed to feed them half a month. And then . . . ?

Our local relief committee made an estimate of $130,000 needed to touch the fringe of the misery around us during the next six months. If summer exchange rates continued, this would mean about $10,000 U.S. But with the more spectacular disaster in Tientsin and widespread needs elsewhere, it was doubtful how much relief could be assigned to our area.

Water was not the only foe. Fields that escaped the flood were visited by millions of ravenous worms that devoured the tender young heads of grain. Cholera broke out in some sections. It was a comfort to send out a remedy which we learned from a visitor from India years ago, but it was too expensive for general distribution.

This was the dark, dark canvas on which God was painting the radiant colors of His love and care. In spite of seeming impossibility, eight bands of young women and two groups of young men were busy in the country all through the summer. They met every kind of difficulty and danger but came through unscathed. Sometimes their escape from harm was by so narrow a margin that their heavenly Father's hand was all but visible. What a thanksgiving meeting they had upon their return home, each bursting with good news of God's wondrous working. We spent a whole day telling and giving thanks.

Only eternity will reveal all that was wrought by the courageous faith and glowing testimonies of these young people. We saw but the outskirts of His ways, but we did know that many who had been fleeing at each rumor came to put their trust in God when danger threatened and had cause to rejoice in His faithfulness.

When the pest of worms was filling hearts with black despair, these fearless young evangelists preached repentance and faith. One man went through his field shaking the worms into a tray. He gathered about a quart. He went through again and returned with a peck. The third trip yielded a bushel and he confessed himself beaten. The evangelist pointed out the futility of human means and urged turning to God in their extremity. And some did, with remarkable results. One man went the whole way and prayed simply that God would have His way with his field. He did not even go out to watch the progress of the pest. "Let God leave me what He wants me to have," was his unworried remark. When the worms had gone, everyone found with amazement that they had stopped just short of this man's field! On both sides was devastation, but his grain was untouched. What an evidence of a loving Father's tender concern for His repentant child.

We had many hindrances to holding evangelistic meetings during that summer. Disturbed conditions prohibited evening gatherings in many places, but in almost every case faith was given to run the risk and always blessing followed. So keen were people to hear the Word that sometimes even a brisk shower would not disperse the crowd, and in some places they stood ankle deep in mud and water to listen.

The lateness of the season crowded the farm work, making it an unusually busy summer. People came dead tired from the fields and yet unwilling to lose the opportunity for Bible study. So the noon rest hour was given over to classes. In the terrific heat this was hard for both teachers and pupils, but about 400 joyfully endured and were repaid from the treasure of the Word.

Probably 1,300 regularly attended meetings and at least 350 of these became new converts. The reality of the experience of some of these put to shame older Christians. One young man was the eldest son in a desperately poor family. They lived from hand to mouth and frequently borrowed from relatives and neighbors to meet their need. When he was converted, the young man—convinced that these obligations must be cleared—subsisted on one meal a day while he turned the proceeds from his weaving to pay these debts. "Starvation can't bar my soul from heaven," he said. "But with this burden of debt upon me I can have no peace now or hereafter." His heroic example made a tremendous impression upon his community and his own father was won to the Lord.

Another man had a startling change as he began to put into practice all that he heard. His transformation was the means of winning his wife. The key to the change in another came with the realization that he must not only confess but leave his sin. One youth with a bad reputation became a shining light. His mother was saved in May and then the boy gave himself wholly to the Lord, enrolling in Bible school to prepare himself to lead the little group in his home village. A woman over seventy heard the gospel on the street while her fingers were busy making a shoe sole. She was saved at once, destroyed her idols, and entered into the joy of the Lord. Others followed her example.

We planned 16 or 20 summer vacation Bible schools as the basis of the summer's work. But the children, busy gathering fuel or spinning thread, did not have time to study. Though many hundreds hopefully enrolled, only about 300 could attend regularly. These received a fine grounding in the gospel and many of them mastered the phonetic script by means of which they could read their Bibles.

In spite of a full schedule of classes and meetings some of the bands found time for home visitation and frequently were invited to help destroy the idols. One woman had 166 to tear down, many painted on cloth. The practical-minded evangelist washed them off so the cloth could still be used for bedding and clothing. The new convert was delighted that she was actually enriched by destroying the false gods that had despoiled her for so long. Now she wore them instead of buying them incense and offerings. Her niece, impressed by her new freedom and joy, destroyed her own gods, too, of which she had a mere 34.

The demand for Bibles continued. I felt like a millionaire when we were able to get in a stock of all sizes, including the ones with phonetic. It was a constant cause for thanksgiving

that the Bible Society was able to supply such beautiful vol-
umes for so little money, and thrilling to get the Word of God
into the hands of those who treasured it and fed upon it.

Sometimes a conversion had startling results, stirring up
fury in the unseen world. A woman was joyfully saved and immediately her daughter became demon possessed. She reproached her mother for breaking with the old ways and threatened all sorts of calamities, even the destruction of her own
life. The girl did jump in a well but was rescued. In the midst of
this trouble, the father was brought to repentance. Together
the parents prayed for their daughter and she was delivered.
The family's witness to the power of God was instrumental in
the son-in-law's salvation also.

In a time when physical suffering was so widespread, it
was life and health to be able to point people to such a God as
ours. One poor blind woman believed. She was in desperate
need and continued in prayer all night. The answer was a little
grant of $4 from a faraway relief committee which reached her
just at that time. This small fund was soon exhausted and again
her only recourse was prayer. But isn't that enough? Why do
we ever wonder? Her husband who had not been heard from
for years unexpectedly returned. He, too, was saved, changed
his prodigal ways, and began to support his wife by his weaving.

Our band this summer was augmented by eight Bible
school girls who had this fine opportunity for practical training
with the more experienced workers. They felt they learned more
than in a whole year of school, and a new burden for the unsaved was put upon their hearts. We prayed that perhaps the
Lord would lead some of them to join the band later. The whole
object of our big Bible school was simply to prepare laborers
for His harvest.

With the opening of the fall semester, classrooms and dormitories were simply bursting. Evidently the good report of
the Lord's working in our midst had been spread abroad and
some fine young women from other missions had come for our

advanced course. In addition to more than 200 in the regular Bible school, we opened an Opportunity School for about 50 others. These were particularly needy girls whom we felt we must help. Their number was limited because that was all we could squeeze into the available space. We were sure the Lord would provide their food. He always had in the past when He put a "must do" upon us. We gave them a simplified course: Bible, writing, and arithmetic in the morning and sewing in the afternoon. I was particularly interested in the sewing, for a good needlewoman has a lifelong resource.

Foreign exchange was in a dizzy state that summer. Every U.S. dollar brought $14, $15, and $17 in local currency. In this way every gift was multiplied like the loaves and fishes—and like the loaves and fishes, the gifts had the Lord's blessing. I'm sure that the givers shared in the blessing even as did the little lad so long ago, and I thank them in the name of Him who has received and used them.

I doubt not that God raised up our little band for such a time as this. When our whole world was being shaken it was glorious to have a testimony that was sure. "I know whom I have believed, . . . and He is able" (2 Timothy 1:12). I prayed that we would be kept faithful.

Map of Florence's three month itinerary
November 1939-January 1940
Over 700 meetings held and 100 baptized

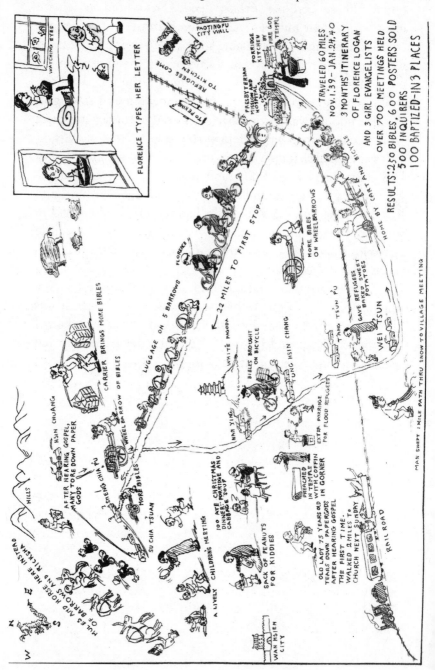

CHAPTER 43

IN THE COUNTRY (1-6-40)

One day I was perched on my bedding roll in a little mud house. Our room adjoined a stable from which the donkey had been temporarily ousted in order that we could use it for a kitchen. But he left his fragrance behind and it still permeated the place!

The big iron kettle—under which we burned bean stalks to cook our food—was temperamental and smoked frequently so we had to open the window to air out. The window, of course, was paper and had some convenient peepholes through which small eyes could peer. It also had a large "eye" higher up for ventilation. When the audience outside became tiresome, we hung a sheet which rudely obstructed the view.

A little heat from the cooking found its way under our k'ang so it wasn't too frigid to sleep upon, but not enough warmth percolated to materially affect the temperature of the room. It was nearing the coldest part of a North China winter but no coal was to be had in the country. When my fingers grew stiff I stopped and warmed them on a hot water bottle.

For a normal breakfast we ate a sort of corn pone made of coarse corn meal and native dates. These "muffins" were plastered along the edge of the iron kettle and steamed, while a bowl of watery millet porridge cooked below. As a treat sometimes we had some fried bean curd bought at the market.

Our suppers were even less complicated—simply corn mush eaten with a bit of salt pickle.

These humble living arrangements and simple fare were enjoyed with great thanksgiving, for there were so many who lacked even this much. Every meal was interrupted over and over again by the cry of a beggar at the gate, "Old lady, give me something to eat." We purposely made a surplus of porridge or steamed some extra bread in order to have something to give away, and each time we heard a cry, we hurried out to give from our abundance.

There were literally thousands from the flooded area who begged from door to door. One day a crowd of them came to listen to the gospel. Some showed evidence of having seen prosperous days, but the ravaging waters had stripped them of everything. I longed to hand them each a dollar but one of my wise colleagues restrained me. "If you start that, we shall be mobbed and cannot stay and preach the gospel." Too true; so we found other means of helping them. Perhaps as we leave we can fling our largess behind us and flee!

Besides these hungry ones, there were thousands who couldn't spend a peaceful night on their own k'angs. They lived in constant fear lest their village be made the target of the big guns, or else that they be carried off for ransom, or for imprisonment and torture. The head men of the villages were in particular danger. Hundreds of them lost their lives or had their homes burned.

Many spent the nights in the fields. One wonders how they endured the freezing cold. Each night as we lay down in peace to sleep, we gave thanks that we had a loving heavenly Father to watch over us, and we longed to bring these others into His family and under His care.

On one particular day, a mob of children outside were reciting at the top of their voices, "The heavenly Grandfather loves everyone and sent His Son to save sinners." In a neighboring home, where I led the morning meeting, a group of girls were being taught the phonetic. We were aghast when we moved here and found we had to hold all services in the yard. But on most days the sun was warm and even at night, in spite of the cold, people stood indefinitely to listen. But we realized a little bad weather would stop the meetings, so we prayed, and a new temple was cleared out for the evening services. It was unheated but it was still a protection from the wind. We prayed that one day it would become a place to worship the living God instead of the hierarchy of dead worthies who were painted on its walls.

The week before, one dear woman, a convert of only a few months, led me to another village to preach. On the way she said, "Miss Logan, you don't know my story; from a small child I have been in a Buddhist cult, burning incense and making merit. There really is a devil, and the more incense I burned the worse he tormented me. He took control of me and spoke through my lips.

"I couldn't get free from him and had spells of insanity. They told me that if I worshiped a whole list of more than 80 names I would be harassed no longer. When a gospel preacher came here last summer, I was determined not to listen for I felt I was in the right way. But the children urged me to go and as soon as I heard, I realized the truth. At first I didn't care to tear down all those idols, but Mr. Hsu assured me there was no danger. I received the Lord and the devil left me and doesn't dare to return. Isn't it wonderful? Oh, it is terrible to be in the devil's clutches."

That morning I had been quite miserable with flu symptoms, chills and aching, but since I promised, I felt I should go anyway. Preaching was an effort, but quite a group knelt to pray and I was asked to tear down a kitchen god. The following Sunday an old woman 73 years old walked three miles to attend church with us. She had heard the gospel for the first time that day, had torn down her idols, stopped burning incense and was trusting the Saviour. While people were constantly turning to the Lord, it was rare for one so old to change so suddenly. That Sunday happened to be my birthday. What a beautiful birthday gift from my Lord! Had I failed to go that day, this dear old woman would undoubtedly never had heard.

We had already been out about 10 weeks without a day of rest, but the Lord gave us strength and kept us well. He also very definitely arranged our itinerary for us. The place that was scheduled as second on our list failed to get in touch with us so we knew the Lord had something better. We accepted an invitation to Su Chia T'suan but before we started, the Hsin Chuang church begged us to go to them first. They had to meet in the yard to accommodate the crowds, so it was important to have us before the weather grew cold. This seemed sufficient reason for changing our plans, yet we could get no peace about it and felt constrained to keep our promise to Su Chia T'suan. Later we found out why we were thus led. We had no sooner moved than a big snowstorm came with days of bitter wind. When we did eventually go to Hsin Chuang, the weather was perfect and the work unhindered. How wonderful to have an all-knowing Father to arrange these details for us!

The work in Hsin Chuang filled our hearts with rejoicing. Many fine people turned wholeheartedly to the Lord. I had the joy of tearing down false gods in many homes. One family that was deeply entrenched in idolatry this time really came clean. What rejoicing that must have occasioned in the presence of the angels!

Forty or fifty gathered each morning for the daybreak prayer meeting. One business woman was beautifully converted. Even the news of her husband's death did not destroy her faith and joy in the Lord. At prayer meeting one morning she said she had been unable to sleep. The Lord had been prompting her to provide a commodious house of worship for the group. We didn't know what this might lead to, but perhaps she could be another Lydia.

As we were busy packing to leave, a wealthy man came to beg me to come to his home. He and his wife wanted to learn to pray. After sending off our stuff and having our farewell prayer meeting with the believers, we went with him. The false gods had already been destroyed and the walls were bright with gospel posters. After making clear the simple way of salvation, we taught them to pray and hurried off on our bicycles to catch up with our baggage.

In the next place, where idolatry was especially strong, we fought against heavy odds. The devil used every means to keep his captives from gaining their liberty. I called in a wealthy home where a son had become interested in the gospel while refugeeing in Paotingfu. A crowd came to listen but in a few minutes a wedding struck up on one side and the piping drew away the eager spectators. Soon an unusually violent fight broke out on the other side with angry voices shouting their grievances. Those who resisted the first attraction were unable to miss this excitement and rushed off to see who would get the best of it. My hostess and one or two others showed marvelous self-control and stayed to hear the gospel. In spite of all this, there were some trophies of grace. We were assured that the Word was still living and would still bear fruit.

As the holiday season neared, we felt rather forlorn at the prospect of spending Christmas in this place where so few believers lived. Then a warm-hearted group in another place announced they were planning a big celebration and begged us to join them as they were inviting the Christians from all around. We were delighted to spend Christmas with these who were celebrating for the first time.

With the perfect weather, meeting in the courtyard was no disadvantage. Fully 300 heard the Christmas message while about 100 feasted together on millet and cabbage soup. They planned to make some special food for us, but I told them we would come only on condition that we might eat just what they did. We provided a flour sack full of peanuts for the kiddies. Friends in Paotingfu sent us so much candy we had enough to distribute to the grown-ups, too, while each child was given a Sunday school card and each adult a Bible verse, making it a festive occasion. Groups from three villages had each prepared a song and the porch which served as pulpit was attractive with colored paper decorations.

We continually were invited to new villages but had to regretfully refuse. One young man, on fire to win his neighbors, invited a young Christian from another village to come. They opened a little chapel where they daily taught the people, but they felt the need of help.

When I went there one day, some of the old women were almost in tears. "Whoever heard the like of this?" they begged. "Teacher, come and stay here a few days." When I promised to pray about it, they said, "You will go away and forget all about us." But we were determined to go back and we prayed that the Lord would liberate them. They were attracted by the love of God but held by fear and superstition. It would take a miracle of grace to nerve them to break with the old and trust in the Saviour.

Goodness and mercy followed us! I had to return home for much accumulated business. Monday we moved to T'ang T'sun P'u and I planned to come in the next morning. But that afternoon after preaching awhile I felt restless and, in spite of a head wind, felt impelled to return at once. It was heavy going and I had no time to spare before dark, but made it safely though very tired. Bath and bed were unspeakable luxuries. The next morning I awoke to a white world and knew why the Lord had prodded me home ahead of time. The snow made roads impassable for several days. What a wonderful Lord!

In Paotingfu the relief work went on faithfully. At the porridge kitchen in the fire-god temple just outside our gate, 1,350 pathetic folk got their daily portion. Still more pathetic were the hundreds who had to be turned away, empty-handed. Available funds would run the kitchen until March 7, and we prayed that funds would come in to continue, for without this meager aid the plight of these people would be desperate.

The 80 girls in the newly opened refuge increased to 100. They had two meals a day and slept on the floor, yet their lot was the height of luxury compared with those outside. Would that we had room for 500! There were at least 20,000 homeless refugees living in old temples in 80 villages around the city. Grain was distributed to them as fast as funds permitted, but what we were able to give was only a drop in the bucket.

One old man begged from door to door throughout three villages without receiving a mouthful. Exhausted, he crouched in the sun near a doorway until someone took pity and gave him a piece of sweet potato. But life can't be prolonged in that fashion. Everywhere people were eating the wheat sprouts which caused them to become terribly bloated. In Paotingfu for months it was impossible to buy flour, and grain of every kind doubled in price.

We stretched pennies by buying rags and piecing them together to make hundreds of suits of winter clothes—veritable Joseph's coats but they kept folks from freezing. Unprecedented spiritual opportunities and unprecedented physical needs faced us. We fell on our knees in prayer.

Chapter 44

A New Band (4-1-40)

Five rifle shots in quick succession spattered the dust on either side of the two girl evangelists. They jumped from their bicycles as several soldiers came running up.

"Oh, they're women. Our mistake. Go on."

They did go on and started meetings in two villages that very night. They were out to buy up the evangelistic opportunities of the Chinese New Year season and had no time for nerves or hysterics.

"Thank God and go on." That was the spirit that carried eight bands of young people triumphantly through three weeks of special preaching missions and, later, nerved five bands to carry on through thick and thin.

From a human standpoint it seemed impossible for work to continue under those conditions. All intercourse between villages was practically cut off. In many places meetings were taboo. Sometimes believers, because of their fearlessness, were accused of being unpatriotic. Then there was the constant process of being ground between upper and nether millstone, spies, suspicion, paying off grudges, and people carried off for ransom or torture. One side compelled a community to pay taxes; then the other side punished that village for giving aid to the enemy. Oh Lord, how long?

But in spite of everything the gospel was still being preached and people were turning to the Lord. Conditions constantly changed. A village that was closed one day might be open for unhindered work a few months later. So the bands traveled in the steps of faithful Abraham and started out, not knowing whither they were going. Their faithful God always prepared a way before them.

February 10 was a memorable day—with seven big carts, two wheelbarrows, and a dozen bicycles loading up to carry eight bands to the country. This was the largest number that ever started out on a single day. Each group had its outfit well organized so there was a minimum of confusion. This required days of busy preparation and planning.

"How many Bibles should we take?"

"How many catechisms will be needed?"

"What will be the probable demand for gospel posters?"

But estimates based on previous experience proved entirely inadequate and practically every band exhausted its supplies before moving to its second place. Bibles! Bibles! Bibles! The Bible houses were unable to print them fast enough. Four times the normal number were sold the past year all over China and the demand continued to grow. This was about the only business prospering in these disturbed times.

The year before a band had worked in one county for several months and scarcely sold a single New Testament. One year later, people in the same place were buying dozens of copies of the whole Bible, and studying it as well. More than once, when the band moved on, the local group pled for a person to be left behind to carry on the Bible study class, but this usually was not possible. Sometimes there was an older Christian nearby who could continue to help them after the band left, but we tried to teach them to dig into the Word for themselves.

Almost every band reported an outstanding example of a leader of an idolatrous cult being converted. These people had been having intercourse with demons for so long that it was difficult for them to get free. But there was power in the blood of the Lord Jesus.

One band had been working in the flood-stricken east field where the land was still largely under water. In some places when it receded, people planted wheat hopefully, then the water returned. The suffering in that district was such that the girls could scarcely endure to eat their own meals with so many hungry ones around them. Their only comfort was that the people's attitude to the gospel had changed. Where formerly indifferent or even hostile, they now really wanted to be saved. Physical distress had at last given them concern for their souls.

At last we had what we had been quietly waiting and watching for: the gift of a band of young men to do the kind of aggressive evangelism in which our Ling Chan Band of young women had been so greatly used of God. It was the Li Ming Evangelistic Band.

Two or three boys had finished Bible school training, eager to win souls and willing to endure hardness, but had family responsibilities. Though it had come to seem easy and normal for the band girls to trust the Lord for their support, was it practical for heads of families to live by the same rule?

Then a special gift arrived. A dear friend, in laying away the body of his beloved wife, felt impelled to buy a less expensive casket and send the difference in price for the Lord's work in China. Surely the One who prompted the gift had a definite purpose in mind. Suddenly it became clear: This must be the provision for starting the Li Ming Band! If so, then the Lord must be working in the hearts of the young men to prepare them for such a step. And so it proved.

But they met obstacles. One boy had another year of Bible school, while the other two were being used in work on the compound and could be ill spared. So they waited and prayed and prepared. Second-hand bicycles were bought, tambourines, a baby organ, blackboard, cooking kit, and other supplies. Then when it seemed they might be free for work after the Chinese New Year, Pastor Ku was asked to take the new-fledged band under his wing and a busy itinerary was mapped out.

In existing circumstances it was almost impossible for young men to move about the country. They ran the risk of being impressed for service by one side or the other. But we claimed the promise in Psalm 31:20—"Thou shalt hide them in the secret of thy presence"—and the band was unmolested. A large door of opportunity opened before them. Once again the Lord had done the impossible and gone forward when it seemed that conditions would force us to retrench. Truly nothing is impossible with God.

We implored friends at home to make their prayers a wall of fire around these young men. If dependent on human protection, they couldn't continue one day. The name of their band meant "Dawn." They felt they were working in the long dark hours just before the dawning of the Son of righteousness, whose coming is our blessed Hope. We prayed for more boys to be called into this work and found four exceptionally fine young men whom we hoped to send on to seminary or Bible school in the fall, most of whom came through our local Bible institute. The regular course only continued for five months each winter, but there was such a demand that we decided to have a two-month course in the spring. The boys carried on Sunday schools in 10 nearby villages. After their New Year vacation, all reported splendid preaching opportunities in their own homes.

The Girls' Gospel School reopened with over 200 in spite of the fact that no students were permitted to come out from certain districts. We had to turn down hundreds of applications, but our prayer was that everyone who had this privilege of study might become a soul winner.

What can I say of the relief work? First, thanksgiving that funds came in to continue our present enterprises and to open two more porridge kitchens. But still hungry stomachs were crying "More, more." The number begging from door to door increases daily. One can satisfy half a dozen with leftovers, but when 20 or 30 come in succession, you must prepare a lot of extra food. Each beggar carries a stick to ward off vicious dogs and a bag to carry the crusts that are given out. Sometimes they have a bowl for liquids, and sometimes a pail.

My heart was especially touched one day to see a well-dressed woman and a little girl with the familiar stick and bag. They obviously came from a formerly well-to-do home but had simply reached the place where gnawing hunger forced them to swallow their pride and take their place with the ragged hordes of beggars. Many who were able to scrape along through the winter were now at the end of their resources and had to beg or starve. Only the more husky ones would survive on such precarious rations.

Already smallpox had appeared in the refugee camps near here, so Miss Atterbury and the nurses who assisted her were busy with vaccination parties.

At Hsin An in the flooded area we were carrying on a class in mat weaving with about 70 women and girls. They were given food for a month while learning. It was hoped that this craft would make them self-supporting, but the market was not very dependable.

We who administered relief needed prayer, for it was hard to be patient and kind when one is almost torn limb from limb by desperate claimants! It was difficult to distribute all there was and then be set upon by hordes of those it was impossible to help. Nor was it easy to be left out! One could not blame them for being desperate.

We repeatedly heard rumors that all Americans would be leaving China. Whether this would be brought about or not is in our Father's hands. We prayed that we would be worthy ambassadors as long as we were permitted to remain. The people at home could scarcely realize what a source of comfort and courage it was to know that so many of them were concerned and praying. They were often in my thoughts, and I had a good time praying for them, each one, as I addressed the envelopes. Sending out a letter was almost like having a furlough and my heart was warmed at each remembrance.

In union there is strength. We needed to be united in faith and love that we could stand in those evil days. We prayed that we would keep looking up at our glorious Lord and go on with buoyant spirit.

CHAPTER 45

MORE BANDS AND GREATER HARVEST
(7-15-40)

How good God was to us! How great His mercies! While opportunities for evangelism were rapidly diminishing, the volume of work done was steadily increasing. This divine paradox filled us with awe. Our atmosphere was vibrant with history in the making and cataclysmic changes were shaking everything we knew, yet with our miracle-working God we faced the future in calm expectancy.

Many country groups that had eagerly pled for summer vacation Bible schools had to later sorrowfully withdraw the invitations. Even their Sunday services could not continue. One would expect our summer work to be seriously curtailed, yet God opened other doors and 15 bands were now at work—a 50 percent increase over last year! Where to find leaders for so many groups? Several of our most experienced workers had been ill and must rest. A serious handicap surely. But the younger members of the band stepped into the breach and courageously led the teams of Bible school girls. They had grown to maturity just in time to meet this emergency. Conditions said "decrease" but God said "increase" and His Word is with power!

So 15 bands went out. While rejoicing in this growth in quantity we were also striving for improvement in quality. We longed to be worthy ambassadors of Him whose name is Wonderful. And the Lord who knew our hearts gave us special help. First, it was possible during the spring to give the Bible school girls who volunteered for this work a course teaching them to use the material selected for the summer classes. For several weeks in June we daily spent hours learning new hymns and gospel choruses. Then, as a climax, the Lord sent to us two precious young women for a series of heart-searching meetings. Thus, fortified and inspired the bands went out with joyful eagerness and expectancy.

When we saw God's hand so obviously moving in our behalf, we confidently expected great things from Him! Not the least of our expectations was that in these days of rampant evil these groups might be kept hidden and secure. One dear Christian woman has recently sealed her testimony with her blood. Her offence was going into the city to church. Should this high honor await us, we had no tears. Our only concern was that Christ be magnified in us whether by life or by death.

The bands that scattered on February 10 were reunited June 2 when we laid our trophies at the Master's feet. It was harvest outside and people were eagerly winnowing the golden grain. We were thankful that the winnowing of our harvest was in the hands of the angels, and we prayed that the precious hoard would be clean and free from tares. There were more than 800 professed conversions reported. The combined Bible classes were attended by 668, while 3565 regularly listened to the gospel message. This did not include the thousands who heard a time or two at fairs and markets.

Prayers were answered for the Li Ming band of young men; they moved in a divinely protected circuit. Often there was serious trouble in a village just before they reached it; frequently there were attacks after they left, but the band never ran into danger. They brought back to Paotingfu an outstanding trophy of grace. He was a real prodigal from a well-to-do family, a boy steeped in evil habits. Cigarettes never left his lips; his passionate temper spared not even his parents. His change of heart stood the test, however. Possessing a bright testimony, he began studying in the short-term Bible school.

The spring temple festivals again gave us priceless opportunities to broadcast the gospel. On one occasion a battle was waged over the head of the panic-stricken crowd. A few were wounded, but the evangelists escaped injury.

I sometimes wished I had more medical knowledge so I might help the sick. But the most skillful doctors sometimes make mistakes, whereas in my helplessness I had a remedy which was never wrong—prayer. I was appealed to for a child in convulsions. The family had heard something of the gospel but were not at all clear about it. I explained the simple conditions for effectual prayer. With the child in such a serious condition there was no opportunity to deal with the mother privately, but prayer was made. The child immediately became normal and wanted to be dressed. The mother, convicted of sin, asked us the next day for prayer.

As we were returning to Paotingfu I decided to distribute what money I had left among the larger families to help them along for a few days longer. We tried to enjoin secrecy, but the word spread like wildfire. Finally we had to rush off in the face of a thunderstorm to escape from the mob. We were drenched to the skin but that was more comfortable than facing those poor people whom we were powerless to help.

Wheat harvest brought blessed relief to most of the countryside. In the mountains where there was no wheat the people ate the trees bare of leaves and still had two more months to endure. Without a little grain to mix with the leaves, at least once in three or four days people become bloated. You can realize how it relieved my heart to be able to send back funds to supply that necessary bit of grain for at least some of the Christian families.

Elements now in power in much of the country boasted of the destruction of all moral standards. Our hearts ached but we did not know yet what the solution would be.

The incessant demands of this year made an unusual drain on our sympathies and nerves. Thank God for vacations! Some who carried the heaviest responsibilities during the year were already away attending a summer conference on the beautiful campus of Yenching University and I was about to leave for a few weeks near Peking. I believed the One who knew we needed rest would give us quiet.

CHAPTER 46

EVACUATION OF AMERICANS (11-25-40)

"Evacuation of Americans"—to home folks a newspaper headline, but to us an uprooting! In a moment life and work turned upside down, or was it not rather rightside up? For were we not called to be pilgrims? We believed the sudden removal of missionary workers was but the tearing away of the scaffolding that the buildings may be revealed. Only the days ahead will show how much was of "wood, hay, stubble" and how much of "gold, silver, costly stones."

Though we made feeble efforts from time to time to evaluate our work, this crisis was doing it for us without partiality. At that time, it was not apparent how soon we would be forced to leave, but the changes and adjustments we were making to prepare for what we expected eventually would have permanent benefit.

Christian leaders formed themselves into a work group, each helping to shepherd the flock as the Lord led. Each worker was to get his guidance directly from the Lord rather than to be appointed to a task by Presbytery's evangelistic committee—a significant change.

One precious bit of gold gleaming through the chaos of ideas was the determination of the bands to stick together and continue to work. "When they persecute you in this city, flee into another" (Matthew 10:23). That was their spirit. And they were full of ideas for maintaining themselves in case they needed to be self-supporting. We knew not what form the Lord's provision would take, but we knew it would be abundant for that is the way of our gracious Master.

The tendency to lean on the foreigner and foreign influence was being cured so suddenly as to be amusing. Ever since the turnover, all sorts of people smuggled all sorts of personal belongings into the compound for safekeeping. All our efforts to get these things cleared out were fruitless. But then hosts of unknown owners suddenly appeared and carried off their precious bundles and boxes, much to our relief!

The government's advice for us to leave came just when we were getting ourselves all fixed for normal life again. Since 1937 we had been getting along with makeshifts; but within recent months we completed extensive repairing of buildings, whitewashing of walls, and other tasks. In fact, the morning the news came, workmen arrived to whitewash our back halls and laundry. In a daze I cleared out the boxes stored there and let them proceed. Facing the prospect of immediate withdrawal, that seemed about as useless an activity as one could imagine. But those walls were now fresh and we could enjoy them every day we remained.

After years of getting along with inadequate facilities, crumbling roofs finally forced us to make drastic changes in our accommodations for country guests and patients who did not require hospital care but also did not need to stay near for daily treatments in the clinic. Other changes made our plant well adapted to the present requirements of the work with the men, women, and evangelistic band. But now? What did the future hold?

I felt like this compound was holy ground, and would some way be preserved for the Lord's work. In 1900, the mission buildings in the north suburb were burned, missionaries and Chinese Christians with them. When the German army came to punish the city, our Dr. Walter Lowrie interceded for the people and saved the place from destruction. In grateful appreciation the gentry and merchants presented this plot of ground to Dr. Lowrie for mission work. So the blood of martyrs and the Lord's forgiving spirit have set this place apart. It is His in a peculiar way; I believe it will be kept if He can still be glorified here.

Supplies have been hard to buy at times, but our missionary families were foresighted and laid in winter coal, grain, and foreign groceries in unusual abundance. The imminence of evacuation turned these stores, once so precious, into a burden. We found ourselves eating them and using them up and giving them away as fast as possible. How startlingly values had changed! Such a grand clearing-out we all had, getting rid of accumulated odds and ends which others might find useful. We were not unduly concerned for our homes and things, for the Lord had kept them for us through so many upheavals, and would do so again if He thought we needed them.

After the first flurry of excitement, everyone settled down to carry on as long as possible, while preparing for any eventuality. No matter how our circumstances changed, we knew the Lord was unchanging. Our anchor held, and quietness and confidence was our portion.

The Ling Chan Evangelistic Band was now in the country, working in three teams; we also left two members to help with city evangelism. The Li Ming Band was out following up some of the new places we opened last spring, and Miss Gould was out with a band of both men and women. Conditions were increasingly difficult and called for greater patience and faith and mighty laying hold on God.

The 15 bands that went to the country in July held summer vacation Bible schools of at least a month in 27 centers. Multitudes of children joyously enrolled, but a pest of grasshoppers descended in many places and the children were called away to chase them off and save the crops. So only about 600 finished the course. In some places the evangelistic meeting started with large crowds but had to stop entirely before many nights. In other cases the meetings began timidly with small groups and gradually grew in size.

But everywhere were called-out ones. A glorious trophy was Mrs. Teng, estranged from her family, living in sin, and bound by evil habits. She sought consolation in nicotine and consumed two packages of cigarettes a day. Life became unbearable and she tried to drown herself, but lost courage. Then she brought $2 worth of opium with which to commit suicide, but before she consummated her intention, the gospel intervened. Her repentance was genuine and she immediately wrote her mother-in-law confessing her faults. In the joy of her newfound faith she learned the phonetic script and was now able to read her Bible. Years before she had buried some money and had never been able to find it. After her conversion she prayed about the matter and immediately turned up the missing coins. She gave $13 to the church as a thank offering.

Sometimes in His providence God permits new converts to be severely tested through sickness, persecution and loss. How His heart must be comforted when He finds one who stands true and is not offended with Him in spite of all. There were some such in recent months.

All the bands worked amidst all sorts of alarms and dangers. Two of the men were under arrest for three days until their good character was established. An older woman evangelist and two schoolgirls had to spend two nights on the boat coming home. It was just a tiny river craft that tied up at the bank at an inn. Things grew black with the thought of what might have been but for the Father's loving watch care. That night soldiers searched the boats for girls. How can we praise Him enough that they were safe ashore! Truly any road is safe when He leads the way.

Our dear neighbors, the Cunninghams, sailed on one of the first evacuation ships. Both had passed their eightieth birthdays and the year celebrated not only their golden wedding but also the fiftieth anniversary of their arrival in China.

Next would be Dr. Mackey who would sail in January for furlough and retirement. The uncertainty of life here made it a bit easier to let her go. The rest of us waited further developments as to the order of our withdrawal.

A deluge of rain in November was very unusual in our dry North China. But such we had, and it gave me a very interesting time trying to get home from the country in time to see the Cunninghams before they sailed—jumping ditches and slough- ing through mud and clambering up slippery banks, dragging my bicycle through it all. I think I carried it as often as it car- ried me, but for shorter stretches. There were friendly folk to lend a hand or give direction in several of the difficult places. I felt all the way that I was being Personally conducted.

During harvest while country people were busy, the bands gave more time to city evangelism and held a class for women inquirers. The eagerness of these new believers to learn to read their Bibles made that a glad time. Before rally we had a day of prayer from six in the morning till six at night, with the leader changing each hour. In the middle of the morning a call came for me. The Lord suddenly reminded me I had asked Him to send folk to me, so I eagerly went to His appointment and found one ready to be led to the Saviour. What if I had been too busy, even with praying!

The country people had had little shepherding in the past year, and in this time of trial, fear and, persecution some had denied their Lord. But the promise is: "I have chosen you . . . that ye should go and bring forth fruit, and that your fruit should remain" (John 15:16). We prayed that we would see souls stead- fast to the end.

CHAPTER 47

NEVER ALONE (3-15-41)

"Well that woman certainly has nerve," chuckled the guard as I pedaled into view on my trusty bike. "Aren't you afraid?" he asked. I assured him that it wasn't my nerve but the presence of the true God that kept me safe and confident. With the country full of violence and bloodshed it was a miracle that I continually traveled back and forth without once meeting any hindrance. Over and over people asked in dismay, "But you're not going alone, are you?" I always replied, "No, the Lord is going with me." And I proved it so. Praise His name!

With the future unknown and breathtaking changes coming overnight, what comfort there was in knowing just such intimate guidance and care from our heavenly Father! Once during the wintertime I had planned to return to Paotingfu on a certain day, but that morning dawned with a snowstorm. While the weather made it impossible to travel or carry on our usual work, it brought in a large group of inquirers for Bible study. We had a blessed time considering the meaning of bearing the cross. At the close, one young man said, "I've never seen it before; this is just what I needed. The Lord kept you here that I might get this lesson."

By noon the storm abated. Did the Lord have further need for me there or should I return to Paotingfu? I put out a Gideon's fleece: "If the snow has entirely stopped by two o'clock, I'll infer that I am to go." It did stop and the wind had swept the highway clean so I had an unusually easy trip home. Arriving in Paotingfu I found my colleagues about to send for me as I was needed for an executive committee meeting. The Lord had kept me in the country long enough to finish the work there and brought me home just in time. When He makes such accurate plans for His most insignificant child, why should we fret and worry?

Great changes seem imminent, but our fresh testimony was our Ebenezer, "Hitherto hath the LORD helped us" (1 Samuel 7:12). For a few days in the fall evacuation rumors threatened to send the Bible school girls scurrying to their homes, but saner counsel prevailed and they finished the term and happily began on their spring work.

"Time marches on." And so did the bands. That winter I had the joy of working in Man Ch'eng county, for many years our despair. Too many unregenerate ones had entered the church for material advantage. But now, praise the Lord, new life abounded everywhere. Humbly, some told how the power of Christ had saved them from definite, loathsome sins. Small wonder many more were moved to trust such a Saviour!

We found a heartwarming response in Tung Tien Chuang. Before moving to this stronghold of Buddhist superstition we had been preaching at a market. One woman simply devoured the messages and was eager to learn to pray. She proved to be from this new village. Her receptiveness gave us faith to believe that the Lord had other hungry hearts waiting for us there, and we were not disappointed. However, the joy of leading them to the Lord was tempered with pain. I had had a precious time teaching and praying with a group of dear women when one asked, "Why didn't God send you to us earlier? Ever since the turnover we have been desperately seeking for security and peace of heart. Knowing nothing else we have been burning more incense, making more vows, performing more genuflections. Oh, if we had only found the Lord Jesus sooner!"

I'm afraid we hadn't been keeping up with God's calendar. We needed to pray that we would catch up, and that the mighty ordination of the pierced hands might be laid on more of the Bible school girls. A class was graduating in June. Would some of these be called?

A goodly crowd, largely from surrounding villages, still worshiped at the Man ch'eng city chapel. Going into town was a trying experience, for everyone entering the city gates was searched and had to bow to sentries. But, in spite of this inconvenience, the congregation pleaded for some special meetings. Accordingly a week of daily Bible hours was arranged. At the close, on their own initiative, ten men signed up to take responsibility for shepherding the small country groups. After morning service at the chapel, they went two by two to lead services in nearby villages. These churches in the homes were the strongholds of the faith but they lacked leadership. Although the volunteers had no special training, they undertook the work prayerfully and the Lord blessed their ministry.

Another band continued the work started last spring opening a new field in Tinghsing county. With no church members to find places for them and few inquirers through whom to make contacts, it was a difficult job of pioneering. In one instance a young believer arranged for them to visit her maiden home. The family extended the invitation rather grudgingly and the room provided was dreadfully crowded. Their sleeping space was so tiny they practically slept two deep, heads and feet alternating. The courtyard was filthy underfoot and the hearts and mouths of those who dwelt there were no better. Only the humility of the cross and the heroism of faith gave the band courage to enter such an uninviting work.

Carrying on work in such discomfort was very discouraging. Quarreling made a living hell; no one wanted the gospel. Days passed with no results. Should the band leave? They wept before the Lord. "We can't go; we are still their debtors," was the decision. The Lord honored their obedience and immediately the tide turned. Various homes with comfortable meeting rooms were opened; people exclaimed that they were beginning to understand. Each day saw miracles of saving grace. When the band did leave, the new believers shed tears as they pleaded for a soon return. "The next time we'll give you large, clean rooms; we'll never let you suffer like this again," they said with contrition.

Through a distant relative of one member of the band an opening was found in Hung Shu Ying. The whole family was saved, including the old grandfather. The change in him was so striking that his daughters-in-law insisted, "The living God has come to our home!" No other explanation adequately accounted for the marvel. The old man had been of an irascible disposition. He continually threatened to dash the brains out of his little granddaughters for there were too many girls in the family. One cannot imagine the feelings in the mothers' hearts when these violent outbursts were replaced by loving solicitude and the grandfather spent hours caring for the babies he had once execrated. After the band left, daily family prayers were started, they sang a song or two, then all knelt and each in turn prayed aloud. This family continued to generously use its cart to move the band from place to place.

Nineteen forty-one marked the twentieth anniversary of my arrival in China. One must check the tendency to be garrulously reminiscent, yet not miss the opportunity to give glory to God for His unspeakable goodness.

These 20 years fall into two periods, the first ten dry and dusty. Perhaps their chief value was in getting grounded in the language and adjusting to living in Chinese style among the country people. Of positive fruitfulness I see very little. But Pentecost marked the opening of the second period when I and a large part of our church experienced the cleansing and quickening fires of the Holy Spirit. At that time the Lord taught us the secret of implicit obedience, and since then God has continually added to the church such as were being saved. These new believers throughout the country were our joy and crown.

In the early days I went about with an elderly Chinese woman, well-meaning but untrained. We preached in a feeble way to the women in their homes, hoping they might eventually be saved. Now what a change! From a simple little Bible school started in that period have come young women who are real comrades-in-arms. The infilling of the Holy Spirit and the example of the Bethel Band taught us how to work. We preached at markets and on street corners and the Lord made sin, repentance, and salvation a reality in the experience of multitudes who were hearing the gospel for the first time.

To one who struggled along in the old isolated fashion, work in the bands was a taste of heaven. A fourfold cord is not easily broken, and there was multiplied strength in a team of four who were one in heart and purpose.

The service given by the bands so commended itself to the country churches that the local leaders worked in beautiful cooperation. They provided transportation and made extensive gifts of food and fuel. The band work was so indigenous that it could go on when more highly organized projects were hindered.

About a year before one of the bands was definitely guided to include an unplanned-for village in its itinerary. Many were saved there. Soon after the band left, that village was cut off entirely from communications with the outside and afterwards became the scene of continuous warfare. But praise to our faithful God, word came that all of the believers were standing true; there was no falling away in attendance at Sunday service, and the Christians experienced many evidences of the Lord's special goodness to them in the midst of so much trouble. The Lord's promise is, "I have chosen you that you should go and bear fruit, and your fruit should remain." How thankful we were that there was a band to do that work just in time. What a tragedy if this opportunity had found us still puttering along as in the old dry and dusty era!

CHAPTER 48

RESTRICTIONS AND PERSECUTIONS (SEPTEMBER 1941)

"Frozen" in midsummer. Thus we missionaries were caught in the world situation and were busily trying to find out all it implied and how we could adjust ourselves to it.

I was in the last week of a delightfully refreshing vacation at Peitaiho Beach when the order went into effect. One of the immediate reactions was the "freezing" of the baggage of Americans traveling back and forth from their holidays. Some of my colleagues checked their trunks and found upon reaching Peking that they were "frozen." About a week of diplomatic negotiations resulted in the rescinding of that part of the program. However, the matter had not been cleared up when I left the beach, so I tied up in a sheet most of the things from my little trunk and carried them as hand luggage. Such a bundle was a common sight in the Orient so it did not excite the interest it would have evoked at home. A few days later a kind German friend brought the trunk to Peking.

There were other scattered instances of American property being "frozen"—guards placed at the gate and nothing permitted to leave the place. At first wild rumors stated that all American institutions had been closed. Chinese staff members living on our compound hastily moved their possessions to places that seemed safer, but we were not picketed.

Our greatest inconvenience was in the matter of money. We were supposed to be permitted a limited sum for living expenses but a plan had yet to be worked out as to how we were to get it. Many missionaries were involved. Personal checks on banks in the United States had to be returned, but cashier's checks could still be handled.

With so much uncertainty about income, most of us were retrenching on our living expenses. We closed our kitchen, pensioned our cook, and doubled up with others in every way possible. I began to take my meals with the evangelistic band girls. That meant a diet such as we had in the country with no milk, fruit, or sweets. Consequently, it was cheap.

After the turnover, restrictions were set up on buying various things. Quite naturally those restrictions were being enforced rather rigidly against Americans. Coal was a great problem since the normal supply for North China now went to the munitions factories of Japan. For our entire compound we were promised about one-third of the amount required by the hospital alone. Kitchen stoves were remade to burn coal dust with the use of a bellows. We had no hope of being able to heat our missionary houses, so we wore mountains of clothes in the winter. It was becoming increasingly difficult to obtain hospital supplies of all sorts; thus, it became rather an exciting game to see how long we could keep going!

Since July 1 it was necessary for all foreigners to have a special military pass for each time they bought a ticket for train or bus. It could take days or weeks to get such a pass, or it could be refused entirely. This added another complication to life in a frozen state.

Returning to Paotingfu I applied for a pass good for six months and was given one valid for six days. I was mighty thankful to get home at all and quite content just to stay put.

The most important consideration was how world politics would affect the Chinese Christian church. It seemed inevitable that much suffering was in store, but the Lord was teaching us that He is able for every situation, so our hearts were at peace. Do those words sound easy? I wonder if you can fathom what they meant during the anxious days in August when three of our bands were in prison. Four of our young men and eight of our precious girls have joined the company of Peter and Paul, prisoners of Christ Jesus.

With what surpassing kindness the Lord led me in June to make no assignments for summer work. The knowledge that each evangelist had definitely felt guided to a particular field was indeed a light shining in a dark place, when three of those fields included imprisonment. The two bands working in Tinghsing county were taken into custody by order of the Japanese Military Police. The chapel in which the men were living, owned by the local Christians, was sealed, and the executive committee of the church was taken to prison also. Ostensibly they were being held for questioning. Held in an office instead of in a jail, they were treated courteously and suffered no hardship. Their friends were allowed to send in food.

The girls were taken to the prison in the county seat and locked in a filthy, dark, vermin-infested room for 24 hours. Thereafter they were given the liberty of the courtyard and, here, too, friends arranged for food to be sent in from an inn. Their Bibles and all their Christian literature was confiscated but otherwise they were treated with consideration. These girls were naturally timid, but in this emergency all fear was taken away and they were able to witness boldly.

When first taken to the prison they were told they would be beaten. Then the officer seemed to relent and said he wouldn't beat them since they were women, but when questioned they must say they had been beaten.

"Would it be all right if we just didn't answer when asked about the beating?"

"No, you must say we gave you a hard beating."

"We are Christians and can't lie. If that is the case, go on with the beating." Praise to a merciful Father. the beating was never given.

These dear ones had been in prison for four or five days before word trickled down to Paotingfu. We immediately tried to vouch for their good character and secure their freedom. But every road to those in authority seemed blocked. Suddenly on the eighth day they were released without explanation and without ever seeing the military police on whose order they had been taken in.

Was pressure brought to bear through some official channel? It hardly seems that it could have been anything that we had done, but rather the Lord's own intervention. As we were finishing supper on August 14 these two bands suddenly appeared and our prayers were turned to praise. We at home had suffered with them from the uncertainty and the distressing rumors that kept circulating. Now we knew from actual experience that His grace was sufficient even for prison.

The third group was seized by the famous Eighth Route Army while they were in the midst of an evening meeting. The young Christian, in whose home they were living, insisted on going with them. They spent the first night in the field and the next morning were taken to a village where breakfast was provided; then they were committed to the care of two men who were to take them to the county headquarters of the Red Army, hidden away in the hills. On the way, shelter for the night, food, or a cart would be requisitioned for them as need required. They were shown not a little kindness and had opportunities to witness. On the third day they reached their destination where they were held for 20 days, being taken along whenever the county government changed its location. They were treated with courtesy, given the same food as the officials, and were daily called in for questioning and exhortation.

To these men who were enduring hardship and danger to maintain China's resistance against aggression, it was unthinkable that young women of such intelligence and ability should be using their talents preaching the gospel when they might be in patriotic service. They used all their powers of persuasion, but the girls steadfastly asserted that their lives had been dedicated to the Lord and they must serve Him.

Meanwhile the local Christians were trying every way to get a letter through, guaranteeing the good character of the girls. Again the way was blocked. Finally word was brought to

Paotingfu, and through believers in another county it was possible to reach them. After winding through the hills for 100 li, the country elders actually saw them. We were greatly comforted when one brought word they were safe and in no personal danger. For again fearful rumors had been clawing at our peace of heart. This faithful elder made a second trip taking changes of clothing and money for food to the prisoners, and a further appeal to their captor. The days crept by as we longed for word of their release. A week and no news. A country Christian was again urged to find out what caused the delay and bring us word. I fairly flew down the stairs but before my eager questions could be answered, there were the girls themselves! It seemed that life could hold no greater joy!

They had walked 40 miles in three days, but they had no words of weariness, only of the marvelous mercies of the way. Not the least of these was the accurate timing of their release: one day later and they would have been caught in a new campaign of the Japanese never-ending "mopping up" operations. Their protection from disease was no less miraculous. Sometimes they had to drink contaminated water. Their food was frequently black with flies before it was given to them. For fear of contracting the dread trachoma they never once used a washbasin, but poured the water on each other's hands. Cholera had just raged through one of the villages they lived in. And yet they came back well! Could any one doubt that God looks after His own?

Prayer was heard in another respect: these experiences would naturally frighten timid believers and cause new inquirers to draw back "but God. . ." We had evidence that, on the contrary, the faith of many had been strengthened.

In spite of these hindrances the report of the summer's work was gratifying. Sixteen teams worked in 27 places, living on an average of one month in each. At the most conservative count 1,215 people listened to the gospel as it was preached each evening or during the noon rest hour. There were 194 professed conversions. In the daily adult Bible classes 356 studied regularly. Close to 600 children attended the vacation Bible schools. Some of the village schools were in session at the same time, so those children were forbidden to attend the Bible school. In other places the youngsters were hounded to attend classes conducted by the Reds. One happy result of the summer's work was that more than 100 women and older girls learned the phonetic and were then able to read. Large numbers of Bibles and Testaments were sold.

Would we be able to return to the country after harvest the next month? We who lived a day at a time could not predict this. The prospect was for more and more opposition. But just when organized evangelistic effort was seeming more and more impossible, the Lord added four precious girls to our Ling Chan Evangelistic Band. One of these was a normal school graduate who was saved here in refugee days and then graduated from the Tientsin Bible Seminary and was teaching in the Bible school this year while our Yuan Chieh Chen went to Tientsin for a year's refresher course. The others have graduated from our own Bible school, two from the upper and one from the lower course. August 27 was a red-letter day for us when we welcomed them into our company.

The Ling Chan Band now numbered 14, slowly growing from three in 1934. We had experienced so much of the Lord's gracious provision in these seven years that we faced the future undaunted by "freezing" orders, knowing our God could spread a table in the wilderness.

School started again, and we were thankful for each one of the more than 120 girls who had enrolled. The only heartache was that some of our finest couldn't return because of financial difficulties. In part of our district crops were killed by the drought. Much suffering was ahead and we would probably be powerless to distribute relief.

CHAPTER 49

HOME AT LAST (9-12-42)

Home again, having circled the globe to get here! My lungs expanded in free air after sharing the repressions of a conquered people for five years. Nosing into New York Harbor in the early dawn of August 25 was an unforgettable experience. Surging up in my heart were the lines: "Breathes there a man with soul so dead, who never to himself hath said, 'This is my own, my native land'?" Homecoming never seemed more significant. Overwhelming gratitude to God for my share in America's freedom and opportunity made me feel a sacred responsibility to preserve that heritage.

My deep concern emboldened me to voice a few impressions: Do we not as a nation need a quickening of our moral sense? I was convinced that we were now at war because greed had dragged our national honor in the mire and supplied Japan with the oil and scrap iron to commit the greatest crime in history. It alarmed me that this continued for four years without arousing the national conscience. I seemed to have returned to an America groggy with booze, kippered with smoke, and flabby with self-indulgence.

After 10 months' famine of papers and magazines we eagerly devoured everything sent out on the Gripsholm. One of the national women's magazines was starting a safety campaign: as many had been killed on the highways during the preceding 18 months as were killed during the 18 months the United States was in World War I. It was suggested that the age limit be raised for licensing drivers, that state road laws be made uniform, etc. But no word about the arch killer, liquor! This seemed unbelievable until I noticed that full page liquor ads were carried. I wondered if liquor's stranglehold on American life was any less fearful than Japanese tyranny! What we needed was not legislation but a moral awakening, a determination that America shall not fall through debauchery as did ancient Greece and Rome. I prayed that God would save us from indifference, and give us national repentance, temperance, and self-control to win this fundamental spiritual victory without which military success will be futile.

But to the headlines of these past silent months: Surely goodness and mercy encompassed our goings these past months. Last fall I was concerned lest my presence should bring suspicion and trouble upon the girls. After much prayer, assurance was given and I went out with Han Ching Fang's band to Liang Yu, a village 13 miles from Paotingfu. We had a fruitful time. On December 7 we were much again in prayer as to whether I should return to Paotingfu to see our two missionary men off for America. Ching Fang was sure I should, so I regretfully left the work. Thus when war burst upon us December 8 (we were on the other side of the dateline) I was home.

The taking over of the compound, school, and hospital by the Japanese sent a ripple of anxiety through the country. Practically all the other bands had to return to Paotingfu—two because the chapels where they were working were sealed, others because people were afraid. But in Liang Yu the work went on without stopping. This was truly one of the "exceeding abundantly above" answers to prayer given by a loving heavenly Father. He made it very obvious that my group had not suffered because of me.

The war completed what the freezing in July had begun: the cutting off of all hope of funds from America. It left scores of Chinese workers stranded, shipwrecked on the faithfulness of God. The faith of many was prepared for the break. They went right ahead with their work expecting God from His exceeding riches to supply their needs while ministering to people reduced to dire poverty.

The country groups responded valiantly. They continued to invite the bands and, in many cases, supplied them with food as well as lodging. I committed them all to our Father and rested my heart on His goodness. Yet I longed to help a little before I left. I didn't worry, but I spoke to our Father about it.

Three days before we left Paotingfu an amazing thing happened: the Japanese insisted on buying three of our pianos. Two belonged to people in America and we assured them we had no authority to sell. They reminded us that they could take them without payment and asked if we wanted the money. The price offered, though below our valuation, seemed quite fair for used pianos. It amounted to U.S. $75 for one and U.S. $150 gold for the other. So here was this amount of local currency to be paid in America in gold! Thinking of the gifts that hadn't come through, I immediately wrote promissory notes for these amounts, and had enough cash in hand to supply a score of workers with several months' living expenses! How gracious of our heavenly Father to let me have that satisfaction just when the pain of parting was keenest.

On December 8 our Chinese colleagues and friends were told it would be a grave offense for them to have any communication with us. Gradually restrictions relaxed and they could see us freely, but for their own sakes we did not encourage them to come in unless they had business.

In preparation for this emergency the Ling Chan Band had for a year rented rooms in the village behind the compound and kept our supply of evangelistic literature and books there. This was to be band headquarters whenever it was impossible to continue on the compound. After December 8 it was to these rooms the girls returned. But living there had unforeseen complications. Since they were of different surnames they had to register as individuals instead of as a household, meaning that each had to pay the assessments and furnish the day labor allotted to a household.

This was prohibitive. So when it became apparent that the Chinese could continue to live on the compound unmolested, the girls joyfully moved back to Tung Lou, the building that had always been home to them. This building had a separate yard in line with our foreign residences, rather isolated from the rest of the compound. For our purpose it was ideally located, for I could slip into that yard without danger of being observed by guards at the other end of the compound. In this way I had contact with the girls and prayer times with them before it was possible for them to come to our home.

Later they scattered to the country again but kept me in touch with the work through frequent letters. Thus, laboring together with them in prayer I scarcely realized I was confined to the compound. Prayer knew no bounds; it freed the heart for long journeyings and wide concerns. When repatriation seemed imminent in the spring the girls kept coming in one or two at a time for little visits. We had precious fellowship.

Repeated reports had about convinced us that we were not included among those traveling with the diplomats and we were settling ourselves to spend the summer in Paotingfu. Then on June 3 we were told we would be leaving June 6! Fortunately our packing lacked only last minute details. There was great divergence in the amount of baggage permitted in different places. Our Paoting authorities generously allowed each of us to take a trunk. Since there were conflicting instructions about what could be done with things left behind, I succeeded in giving all but my books and papers to my Chinese friends. My simple furniture had served me well for 20 years and I preferred to have it doing some good rather than relying on the uncertainties of indemnity later.

We not only disposed of our own things but ransacked all the unoccupied residences as well; everything that could be used by our Chinese colleagues we gave to them.

Our leaving was not such as we would have chosen: a police escort to the station, and there Japanese officials instead of our beloved colleagues to see us off. A few faithful souls could not be deterred from going, but we did not feel free to have much talk with them. Our hearts were full, especially as we knew that if Japan retained control of North China we would never be allowed to return.

When we left, the hospital was still running with our own staff, but fearful of what changes the future might bring. We left the school stripped of all Christian teaching but with our old faculty still employed. We left the church rising to self-support but forced into a union organization which could be a noose about its neck. We left most of the band members at work in the country with faith and courage to continue in the face of every difficulty. And we left our hearts, wrapped up in the fate of our beloved colleagues and friends.

From Paotingfu we were taken to Shih Men, an industrial city south of us which the Japanese were developing and modernizing. We were kept for a week in a nice Chinese inn. After a few days we were given arm bands and allowed to go on the street unaccompanied. On June 12 we were taken to Peking on the night train, sitting up all night in third class. At the Peking station we were heavily guarded and no one was allowed to speak to us. From Peking we had third-class sleepers which were comfortable.

In Shanghai we were kept on the train until the station was cleared, then taken by bus to the Columbia Country Club which the American Committee had prepared for us. The large halls, social rooms, bar, and bowling alley were all turned into dormitories. Three hundred fifty repatriates were housed there. Aside from the mosquitoes we were comfortable.

After two weeks delay we were given a two a.m. rising gong on June 29, breakfasted at three a.m., and at 4:30 were loaded on buses and taken to the dock. All details of our departures were managed with smoothness and efficiency—the issuing of health certificates, examination of baggage, assignment of staterooms, and so on. Before nine a.m. we were having another breakfast on the Conte Verde. It was a beautiful vessel; even those of us down in third class were comfortable. We had the run of the ship, good food, and excellent service. A special delight was the Italian seven-piece orchestra that gave glorious concerts each evening. We anchored off Singapore for three days to take on oil and water. The Asamu Maru joined us there and we continued the journey together. It felt pleasant to have company across the watery waste of the Indian Ocean.

On July 22 we reached Laurenco Marques and had the thrill of setting foot on the Dark Continent. Here we found a beautiful modern city with broad boulevards and open squares; the climate and foliage were similar to California. It was a thrill to be transferred to the beautiful Gripsholm and to be out from under Japanese jurisdiction at last. The first day we were served a buffet luncheon on deck while the interior of the boat was being cleaned. Did any food ever taste so good? We were given luxuries we had forgotten existed: cold turkey, olives, fruit salad, lettuce! The stewards were amazed at the amount we stowed away.

After two weeks bucking headwinds in the South Atlantic we reached Rio. From there the homestretch was increasingly exciting, culminating in our tying up at Jersey City just across from lower Manhattan. This gave us several days to adjust to American air while waiting to be examined and cleared by customs, army, navy, immigration and the F.B.I. All were thorough but courteous and kind.

At noon August 27, I stepped past the barrier and was a free agent for the first time in nearly nine months. No mail had been permitted to be sent aboard so I couldn't rest until I had collected mine at the Board rooms. How unspeakably precious those first letters were! I felt such loving gratitude for the prayers of many that had brought us triumphantly through the past months.

CHAPTER 50

AWAITING RETURN TO CHINA (8-29-45)

With events happening so rapidly, I knew that any plan or program could become obsolete overnight.

When the threat of civil war seemed less acute, we thought perhaps it wouldn't be long before exiles—Chinese and missionary— could return to their old homes. I felt that the greatest evangelistic opportunity of our generation awaited us. Hearts were open before we left, only war conditions made it possible to reach many of them. Letters a year ago indicated great hunger among the scattered believers. Can anyone wonder that I was impatient of a day's delay in getting back to my job?

But it would be some time before passports and travel facilities were available for women. Only after long deliberation could workers be sent in for specified pieces of approved work.

It was gracious of the Lord to make the waiting time profitable by giving me the chance for some refreshing Bible study at Biblical Seminary in New York. I was thrilled at the prospect of digging into the Word anew. If I was to be counted worthy of having a share in the ministry again over in China I would need the best preparation possible.

At last the departure time came. It was hard for me to leave my father in his frail health. But with his usual sweet spirit, he was unwilling for anything to hinder the Lord's work. He and my mother had moved to San Francisco to be near my sister Lorna, who was with the Donaldina Cameron House in Chinatown. They were having a great time learning to fold themselves away in an apartment, and we were glad they no longer had the care of a big house although it felt strange not to have the home on Queen Anne Hill which was ours for 31 years. In our hearts Seattle still is home.

Our wonderful Lord's word from my Chinese Bible that morning was "Blessed are all they that wait for Him!"

CHAPTER 51

BACK AT LAST (11-22-46)

"Days of heaven on earth" is the only way to describe my unspeakable joy upon reaching war-torn North China and being reunited with my beloved Chinese friends. The months of waiting and uncertainty in Shanghai seeking transportation north all were now forgotten in the satisfaction of actually being here.

Travel conditions made it impossible to let folks know just when to expect us, so some of my girls had been meeting every train for four days. Then what a hilarious reunion! Our fellow passengers on the street car smiled sympathetically at our exuberance. We could scarcely realize our dreams had come true, and we were together again. One of the band leaders, Hu T'sai T'ing, went with me to Tientsin to look after baggage and visit friends.

The joy of reaching Paotingfu was still in the future. Trains ran part of the way but there were almost daily skirmishes along the line. Meanwhile I was pressed with many urgent invitations to spend weeks or months helping in various places both in Tientsin and Peiping.

Humanly speaking there was much excuse for pessimism; inflation was terrific; all outside the cities were enslaved by communist tyranny; internal peace seemed remote. But I found my Chinese friends were living above all this. They had gone through fire and come into a wealthy place where their eyes were wholly on the Lord. Their quality of life filled me with amazement and admiration. They actually submitted every detail to the Lord, seeking His mind through the Word and prayer. Having found it, they confidently expected Him to work miracles—and He did.

I do not know that this was true of the whole Chinese church, but it did describe those nearest to me. They had learned that the church's only problem was workers. Once they were clean, obedient instruments, there was no limit to the work the Lord could do in a short time. So they dared to take time— weeks or even months—quietly waiting on the Lord for His cleansing and empowering. Then when He sent them forth, something happened. I felt that perhaps the seed was here for a worldwide spiritual revival.

We could buy anything, but prices were astronomical. So I was grateful for everything my kind friends gave me to bring along. Each item seemed to fit a special need.

Seven of us, representing four missions, traveled together from Shanghai. On the day I settled the bill bringing our 56 pieces of baggage and freight from Taku Bar (our North China port) to Peiping, I calmly handed over $1,193,600 in cash (mostly thousand dollar bills). They wanted me to wait while it was counted, but I fled to catch a bus. (In U.S. currency this represented about $250 which was quite a bit of money.)

I prayed that I would be worthy of the privilege of being here, also that the countryside would be liberated and the gospel freely preached once more. We likewise asked for new life for those deluded by communism.

CHAPTER 52

RETURN TO PAOTINGFU (4-10-47)

I was "home" and thrilled and grateful to the Lord for permitting me to return. I waited two months in Peiping for the railroad to reopen, then finally came down by truck. Trains were running regularly, though slowly, over new road bed and temporary bridges.

Four of the Ling Chan Evangelistic Band members were waiting for me, a little thin and worn, but triumphant in spirit. Each had a marvelous testimony of God's faithfulness. Twelve of the group of fourteen which I left in 1942 had continued to serve the Lord through these years, walking with Him through hard places and learning deep lessons of trust which they now taught me.

When communists made country work impossible, all the evangelists had to move into crowded rooms in the city chapel. As food became scarce they concealed their lack from human eyes, so when gifts were received they knew they were from the Lord, for only He was aware of their need. The past fall when they moved back to the compound they busily gathered leaves for winter fuel as coal had been almost unobtainable. They also picked apricot leaves to eat. That was their chief "vegetable" when I arrived. What a satisfaction to see them rejuvenated now that the gifts of many had made it possible for them to have proper food again.

During the years of scarcity they were greatly helped by two poor women, one of them blind. These friends gathered dry grass and sifted coal ashes for bits that could still be burned, and took these offerings in to the band members. I suggested that now they might help these women from their tithe. To my amazement they said, "Oh, no! The tithe belongs to the Levites [those who give full time service to the Lord]. We help the poor from the second tenth." In their poverty they had been giving away two tenths, and sometimes much more, of everything they had received. They had nothing and yet were rich indeed!

Things which I gave them to use or sell they hid from the Japanese and saved, sometimes at great risk, in order that I might have them to use when I returned. We had a very cold winter with almost no heat so I was grateful for the fur-lined coat they kept for me. I felt unworthy of such selfless devotion. They also took great trouble to preserve great quantities of evangelistic literature which was now simply priceless, as it was now impossible to get a new supply.

Not only the band girls but all the mission evangelists had grown tremendously during these years. When workers in other missions "forsook him and fled" into business and government jobs, our group continued faithfully to preach through all kinds of adversity. Because of inflation, mission funds that formerly supported a dozen workers were now adequate for only three or four. To meet this situation the evangelists formed themselves into a band and all worked without salary. Mission funds and gifts from friends were shared equally. What inspiring colleagues!

CHAPTER 53

STILL HERE AND STILL FREE (7-23-48)

One day our Lord allowed us to pass through one of those precious experiences when we were sure of nothing but His loving faithfulness. A week before, the road between us and Peiping was thoroughly cut to pieces, all the important places taken by the Reds. Expecting this attack, defense preparations were pushed feverishly. All buildings between the moat and the city wall were razed. Soldiers invaded our compound and built pillboxes along the north and west walls.

We spent much time in prayer and received gracious assurances of the Lord's mighty undertaking for us. So our hearts were peaceful and our minds stayed on our miracle-working God. Can you imagine how inexpressibly blessed it was to pass a night unbroken by the hideous racket of guns? Each morning after a quiet night we were filled with adoration and praise.

Meanwhile we kept busy with the work for which we believed the Lord was keeping us here. At that time we were in the midst of a 10-day "troop school for Christian soldiers"—a lively vacation Bible school with more than 300 youngsters. Most had had no contact with us or the gospel before, so they were a virgin field. One classroom was bursting with almost 100 little first-year girls, so we gave emergency training to 10 older students, entrusting each with a group of 10 which she taught out in the open air.

August 9, 1948. We were still here and still free! There was no explanation except a prayer-answering God. The road was not yet open but occasional military planes took mail in and out. The future was uncertain. But when Moses was faced with the staggering task of leading a nation out of bondage he prayed, "Show me now thy way, that I may know thee." And

God answered, "My presence shall go with thee, and I will give thee rest" (Exodus 33:13-14). Taking that promise for ourselves, we rested and He showed us that His way was to do the humanly impossible. What glorious encouragement when things looked so dark!

Our child welfare center had reopened after vacation, taking in only the most desperately poor. All were noticeably thinner. Word had come that we could expect no more funds from the American Advisory Committee and our present supplies would only last about one more month. So unless the Lord sent aid from some other source, both the child welfare center and the girls refuge would have to close.

The mission made plans for reassignment of North China workers to stations further south, but I felt that each of us needed to receive definite guidance about leaving. For the present I was sure this was still the place of the Lord's appointment for me, though I had no illusions about being able to continue to work under a change of regime. Until then, there were many to be comforted and saved.

At the end of June I went to Peiping for a few days, my first visit to the city for more than a year. It was delightful to see missionary and Chinese friends, but I was eager to get back before summer rains or fighting made the road impassable. In those days the trip included a day by truck and half a day by train, but it was accomplished without too great discomfort. On the way up we came within a few inches of a land mine; we had to back up and detour. A little later we drove blithely over a rope which a soldier was looping around a land mine preparatory to exploding it, but I reached home safely. Then the rains came, and a few days later the fighting!

Inflation continued to run wild; prices almost doubled overnight. It was frightening. But actually an American dollar bought twice as much as it did a year ago. So every gift did double duty and we were grateful to all our dear givers. We were living dangerously, yes, but restfully and expectantly!

CHAPTER 54

PEACE AMID CONFUSION (11-12-48)

Throughout the night the rumbling of trucks told us that the city was being evacuated. Miss Witmer, the hospital nurse, and I were the only Americans remaining. It was a time of great confusion, but our hearts were at peace. Ten days ago, in response to repeated telegrams urging us to leave, we started packing but became convinced that it was a mistake. The Lord had removed the dread and we looked expectantly to see the mercies of our wonder-working God.

Yesterday a few of us went through the city distributing tracts and a word of testimony to every store. People were so distraught that they welcomed every ray of hope. We prayed that the Lord would work in their hearts and bless this last gospel appeal. We could not understand, but perhaps this great suffering was necessary to bring men to repentance. The hours, days and nights spent in prayer were not in vain. Though we were closed behind the bamboo curtain of silence, God had not given up, and neither must we.

The future was entirely uncertain. Treatment had varied in different places. If we were not looted, we would have enough food and fuel to last through the winter.

Usually the first months under Red regime are a "honeymoon" period. The spying, public trials, and punishments come later. We heard, however, that a more moderate group was to control North China. Our confidence was in the promises of God, who filled our hearts and minds with the peace that passes understanding. He was keeping us here for a purpose which was not yet clear.

Not receiving any mail for six weeks, I tried to send out messages in Chinese by "underground." Thank God we could still communicate by way of the Throne! I felt that the coming of our Lord was drawing near and the day of joyous reunion may not be far away. Meanwhile, it was a privilege to be here with these faithful Chinese friends. We kept singing Psalm 146 to a beautiful Chinese tune. It seemed to have been written especially for us!

PART 3

1949-1951

Florence Logan's two-and-a-half year interment in a Communist compound under a completely Marxist regime.

CHAPTER 55

IN ISOLATION
(WRITTEN CONFIDENTIALLY, JUNE 15, 1949)

For almost a year we lived in isolation. When an occasional letter got through by roundabout ways it was cause for great rejoicing. We kept hoping some of ours would get out. Trains now ran to Peiping for which we were grateful.

Though longing for communication to be opened with the outside world, we were more concerned about our heavenward communication, for only supernatural power was sufficient for this new day. Knowing this power was available through prayer, the evil one used every means to keep us from our knees. Our morning study of 2 Chronicles 20 moved us to spend the rest of the day in fasting and prayer.

We were now living in a world that was aggressively anti-God and actively anti-American, among people completely ignorant of the church and its purpose of saving men from sin. Because most of our buildings were used by a large military hospital, we were crowded into a corner. We were not allowed to preach to outsiders or to teach youth.

What a tremendous challenge these conditions presented! Ours was the opportunity to show to a hostile world the love of God through our lives. We needed to let His power be so manifested that the reality of His presence among us could not be denied. Who is sufficient for these things? "I thank God, through Jesus Christ our Lord."

Besides the large frustrations there were thousands of small irritations calculated to destroy our peace and make us spiritually ineffective. Engaged in a terrific struggle with satanic powers, we silently sent out an S.O.S. call for friends to labor in prevailing prayer for us, knowing our God would triumph and we would all share in the joy of that triumph.

It was hard for those in power to believe that an American could be a friend and not an enemy. Students and others were told that it was not advisable to have contact with Americans. The study of English had been almost completely dropped from the curriculum. The whole population was thoroughly organized; everyone was studying communism and being trained to become political agents. Students were required to report daily on one another, whether especially friendly with another, or whether engaged in a small dispute, or whether interest had been shown in some subject. By the same token, workers were asked to spy on one another and accuse one another of real or imaginary faults.

The government promised protection to those foreigners who minded their own business and did not interfere with their program. So, in order to avoid suspicion, I stayed at home, seeing only those who came to me. For the same reason I wrote few letters. Each week I conducted a children's meeting, a women's meeting, and a Bible class, all for Christians. Then there were daily opportunities for helping individuals. How I thanked God for faithful praying friends!

Chapter 56

Respite in Peiping (7-9-49)

Letters from home! I hadn't realized how starved I was for them. But now that the first had come after months of silence I found myself reading them over and over, devouring every word.

The world had changed, but not the mercies of our God. After 14 months in Paotingfu, where Miss Witmer was the only other American, I was now in Peiping, thoroughly enjoying the fellowship of missionary friends in this fascinating city. I arrived on August 19 and my travel permit allowed me to stay until September 26.

Even here the missionary group was greatly depleted. After my primitive living conditions in Paotingfu, an American home with easy chairs, rugs, reading lamps, Frigidaire, and bathroom seemed luxurious and refreshing. Homeside food was a pleasant change and here in the city I could wear foreign clothes again.

But my roots were still among my Chinese friends. As often as possible I went at seven a.m. to join them in two hours of Bible study and prayer. We had been going through Job and the general epistles. I never realized before how much of the Word deals with suffering. Over and over the prayer is voiced that we may gladly suffer for our Lord and not need to suffer for our own faults. It is often easy to confuse the two.

After breakfast together we made trips to famous beauty spots—the North Lake, the palaces, the Temple of Heaven. In each girls' deepest interest was to find quiet places for prayer. They were thrilled with the stately altar of heaven. It was a most satisfying experience to kneel with them in an out-of-the way spot beside the altar and pray to Him whom the builders of the altar had recognized but dimly. At the spot where the emperors placed their hands on the flawless sacrificial animals, confessed the sins of their people, and prayed the forgiveness of heaven, we placed our hands by faith on the spotless Lamb of God and claimed the efficacy of His blood for the millions still in sin and unbelief in China. I had visited this inspiring spot many times. But I confess with shame this was the first time I had fallen on my knees there to pray for those who knew not how to pray for themselves.

Soon I had to return to my quiet life in our noisy compound occupied by a military hospital. Though crowded and handicapped we were thankful our evangelistic group had been able to stick together. We prayed for the wider door for the gospel but meantime longed to make more effective use of the opportunities we had. But I knew my greatest work was prayer. It was also the most difficult and most hindered by the enemy. The pressure from a God-rejecting world on the outside, dissension and fears within, sent us to our knees to claim the Lord's promise of a glorious church without spot or wrinkle.

The name of our evangelistic band meant "Spiritual Warfare." Not only we, but all Christians in the years to come, are on the firing line in a desperate struggle with the great enemy of souls. He attacks body, mind, and spirit, trying every means to make us ineffective. Prayer, yours and ours, will decide whether or not we overcome.

In the spring, when no mail had come for a long time, I needed very much to know whether any gifts were available to send some precious young people on to Bible school. I didn't dare to write a check until I knew that something had been deposited. Then a single foreign letter came, a bank statement, the first I had ever received! How it came is a mystery. The Lord knew I needed that information and it came in time so the students were not delayed. Praise His Name!

What joy to be a servant in the fellowship of the Crucified One!

CHAPTER 57

IN HONG KONG, BUT SOON TO BE HOME (4-12-51)

Oh, praise the Lord with me for His great loving-kindness! "Personally conducted" describes my journey from the other side of the Bamboo Curtain. Never had I realized so deeply how blessed it is to put one's trust in Him. Without hurry or worry He arranged each detail and added to many "and besides" joys along the way.

After waiting three months for a travel permit, Miss Witmer and I left Paotingfu March 22 for Tientsin. On April 4 we sailed on a Danish boat and reached Hong Kong on April 12. Having stayed within our compound walls for 18 months, this change of scene was refreshing! All this time I had been without radio, newspaper, or magazine, so I was starved for news of the rest of the world. Like Rip Van Winkle, I needed a re-orientation course to prepare me for normal life again.

How thankful I was that I left China without a single unpleasant experience. Wasn't that a miracle of loving-kindness? I am sure it must have been the prayers of many forming a wall of fire around us that kept us in peace.

The one hard thing is that now I was separated from my Chinese colleagues and we could not exchange letters. But intercourse by way of the mercy seat never fails. We have had such blessed fellowship on our knees these past years, and my Chinese friends have been such a great inspiration.

Now they faced the future with high courage, concerned only that Christ may be magnified in them whether by life or death. Some were finding new ways to witness. One well-educated young man, after a year of Bible seminary, learned the cobbling trade. Carrying his tools from a pole over his shoulder, he traveled about the country on business for the King. A young woman evangelist took a midwifery course and was eagerly welcomed by country churches. Another carried her stocking-weaving machine on the back of her bicycle and combined weaving with preaching. They needed the wall of fire!

I sailed on the "President Wilson" May 8 and reached the Golden Gate on May 26. How wonderful to renew contacts and visit without police restriction. How I prayed that this freedom would be preserved. I coveted everyone's prayers that the lessons learned these years would make me more usable in God's great program.

CHAPTER 58

OBSERVATIONS FROM SAN FRANCISCO (12-12-51)

How wonderful to be in a land where letters may come and go without fear!

Although enjoying the amazing bounty and freedom of America, my heart was still on the other side of the Pacific. My comfort was that through prayer I could continue to work behind the Bamboo Curtain. I didn't dare bring my prayer list out with me, but gradually have recalled over 500 names of Chinese friends for whom to intercede.

Having seen armies turn back in answer to prayer, we were shocked when the communists finally triumphed. One asks "Why?" A Chinese friend had the answer: "God is permitting this for our own good." He felt that we as Christians needed greater humility and love. Perhaps God was showing us that our foes were not flesh and blood but spiritual hosts of wickedness. If we are not overcoming sin—personal and national (selfishness, pride, intolerance, dishonesty)—then a military victory would be meaningless.

The Word of God and prayer are the weapons of our warfare. Satan today is attacking men's minds, robbing them of the power to think for themselves. In China he was seeking to make the church destroy herself by accusing her own leaders of imperialistic sympathies. Any man so denounced was neutralized; no one dared work with him again. The pressure was diabolically subtle and deceptive. But the promise, "Resist the devil and he will flee" still applied.

My hope was that whereas hundreds of us had been withdrawn from China, we would be replaced by thousands on their knees on this spiritual battle line. At the Christmas season I prayed that we would not only receive God's gift of His Son, but with Him also the "all things" freely given, including the faith, hope, and love we need for spiritual victory!

CHAPTER 59

ASIA AGAIN—A NEW OPPORTUNITY!
(6-18-52)

Here it was—the answer to prayer for guidance about future work! The marvelous loving-kindness of our Lord was giving me another opportunity to serve Him in Asia. I was scheduled to sail in August for Formosa (strike permitting) under our Presbyterian Board of Foreign Missions for work with the Canadian Mission in Taipei.

This leading was confirmed by an invitation from the Synod of the Formosan Church to teach in their Bible school and work among the Mandarin-speaking people on the island. Because I felt I could only return to Asia on the invitation of Asiatics, this opened the door. With a deep sense of unworthiness I prepared to enter.

The old missionary will be a new one again as everything but the language will be unfamiliar. The semi-tropical climate, hot and wet, may be wearing. I will be living and working with strangers. But I am assured that the same faithful Lord will be sufficient for the new situation. Hearing thrilling reports of the evangelistic work the Canadians have been doing, I know it would be a privilege to be associated with them.

Since I had left everything in China an entire new outfit would have to be prepared. My only Chinese friend in Formosa wrote that a refrigerator was the most important thing to take as import duties were prohibitive on anything sent in. I must take with me everything that I would need for five years. I hoped that all my "afterthoughts" would be sufficient for the days to come.

Having been conditioned by two-and-a-half years in Communist China, it was with the utmost reluctance that I brought myself to buy anything. But things necessary for health and effective service are a must, so I shopped and studied the Montgomery Ward catalogue for visual aids, child evangelism materials, insect control equipment, and so on. I also hoped to get a camera and take many Kodachrome slides of the new field to show when I returned. One must try to visualize enough thin cotton dresses for five years of hot weather, and try to find them in this nylon age. I would be busy until sailing time!

So many helped to make this furlough a happy one. Thirteen weeks speaking in the churches of the Northwest was a particular joy. My sister and I drove to the Midwest in May. The beauty of the country and the precious fellowship with some of our supporting church groups made it a memorable vacation and left me refreshed and eager to begin my new assignment.

The changeless Word of God was an antidote for the unrest and uncertainty of our time. What a privilege to teach it! I counted heavily on the prayers of friends at home that we might buy up this opportunity before the night comes and it is too late!

I remain, in the glorious fellowship of the gospel, Florence Logan.

Final note: After ten years of further mission service in Formosa, Florence Logan lived in retirement in San Francisco with her sister, Lorna Logan. While still teaching Bible classes and receiving Christian friends, Florence continued to be an inspiration to all who knew her. On March 2, 1997, at the age of 100, she went to be with the Lord she had served so faithfully.

Florence Logan
(honored at reception)

Order Form

Postal orders:
Patricia Young, 15 County Road 3777-7938, Farmington, NM
87401

Telephone orders: (505) 327-1962

Please send *China My Love* **to**:

Name:_____

Address:_____

City:_____ State:_____

Zip:_____

Telephone: (_____) _____

Book Price: $10.00 in U.S. dollars.

Sales Tax: Please add 7.0% for books shipped to a New Mexico
address.

Shipping: $4.00 for the first book and $1.00 for each additional
book to cover shipping and handling within US,
Canada, and Mexico. International orders add $7.00
for the first book and $3.00 for each additional book.